CU00406549

ISBN−13: 978-1979711494

CONTENTS

"When I used to come here as a young supporter it felt like I was coming to a party every game. I'd leave here, I was brought across to Baird's Bar with some lunatics (laughs) you know what I mean ... it was incredible, incredible ... but it felt like a party.

Turn up here, the team was playing attacking, vibrant football and afterwards it was great. And then you'd go home and talk about it for week. If we can get that going, whether it's a European night, Scottish game, whatever. We need to get the stadium going again."

Brendan Rodgers, 23rd May 2016
Speaking to Celtic supporters at his first media conference

Over 13,000 Celtic supporters turned up at Celtic Park on a sunny and warm Monday afternoon - yet there was no game on. There had been a number of candidates to replace Ronny Deila as Celtic manager including Davie Moyes, Roy Keane, Stevie Clarke and even Henrik Larsson. Yet there was no doubt who the overwhelming favourite for the job was among the support.

An announcement had been made three days earlier identifying the new manager. A press conference had been called for the Monday afternoon to introduce the new manager to the media – and the fans. Thousands of supporters turned up to get a first glimpse of Brendan Rodgers, the new manager of Celtic.

There were so many supporters present on The Celtic Way that the club decided to open up the Main Stand. As the fans kept coming in they overflowed into the Jock Stein and Lisbon Lions Stand. Over 13,000 were present in the ground. It was a welcome like no other in Scottish football.

The Irishman, from Carnlough in County Antrim, was up front about where his loyalties lay: *"I have followed Celtic all my life and to be given this fantastic opportunity and to be part of such a truly great football club is a dream come true."*

He was in no doubt about the job that lay ahead: *"The Club has been in magnificent shape in recent years and has collected silverware regularly during this time. My objective now, of course, is to continue this work, to keep us at the top and again make our mark in Europe."*

Us. He said 'Us.' He's one of Us.

The Scottish Cup Final is deadlocked at 1-1. The game is in injury time and the 91st minute has just started. There are only two more minutes before the final whistle – and what looks like inevitable extra time. Tom Rogic receives a pass in the Aberdeen half. In front of him are Roberts, Griffiths and Sinclair – all marked. O'Connor comes to meet him – Rogic jinks then beats him for pace and drives into the box. Considine stands in his way but the Australian – juggling the ball between his feet – glides past him.

He's ran almost 40 yards and now only goalkeeper Lewis is between him and the goal. It looks like he's slightly over-ran it, the angle doesn't favour him. His right foot stretches to connect with the ball as Lewis starts to dive. From Row N in Area G1 of the Celtic End it looked too tight an angle. The ball went past Lewis but was it going inside the post?

If it's in, Tom Rogic has secured not only a Treble for Celtic, for only the fourth time in the club's history, but it would mean that Brendan Rodgers' team had gone the entire domestic season – 47 games in total – without being defeated. The title of 'Invincibles' would be ours, an incredible achievement and a glorious end to the most memorable Celtic season in a lifetime. *If* it's in.

CHAPTER 1 — JULY
You came home to lead the Green & White

BRENDAN RODGERS
BRENDAN RODGERS
YOU HAVE HEARD US
CALLING IN THE NIGHT

BRENDAN RODGERS
BRENDAN RODGERS
YOU CAME HOME
TO LEAD THE GREEN & WHITE

'Home' called Brendan Rodgers. Celtic Park evoked great memories for him of youthful visits to Glasgow, but it would take some time for the new manager to experience the thrill of his own Celtic eleven running out onto the Paradise turn.

Pre-season took Brendan and his squad to Slovenia and Austria. Charlie Mulgrew and Anthony Stokes had left for Blackburn Rovers (after the Dubliner had helped end Hibernian's Scottish Cup hoodoo with an historic last gap win over Rangers in May) while Colin Kazim-Richards moved to Brazil (presumably to team up with Rafael Scheidt) and his fellow striker Carlton Cole had his contract terminated. It was no surprise that there was no place for these older professionals in Brendan's brave new world.

Some of the 13,000 crowd that turned out to welcome Brendan Rodgers to Paradise

The first major signing was the exciting French teenage forward Moussa Dembele whom Brendan persuaded to sign up after his contract ran out at Fulham (meaning Celtic only had to pay a development fee). The joint attraction of working for the former Liverpool manager and Champions League football were decisive factors in moving north. On the same day it was announced that Stefan Scepovic was leaving the club to join Getafe after a disappointing spell where he scored only four goals in two seasons. He never did make up for his father having scored the decisive goal for Partizan Belgrade against Celtic in the infamous 5-4 game in 1989 which knocked us out of the Cup Winners' Cup.

The capture of Dembele did not impress the denizens of Scotland's sport media. Of course, their dream of a viable challenge to Celtic's domestic dominance would now, they thought, be realised by the long-awaited appearance of The Rangers in the Premiership, after a significant delay in their fabled 'journey.' Now guided by Mark Warburton – amusingly dubbed 'Warbiola' by The Gullibillies due to his achievements in the pressure cooker that is the Scottish Championship – this new version of Rangers had all the arrogance and self-entitlement of the old one.

The Ibrox club of course enjoyed the same subservient coverage from the Laptop Loyal as their previous incarnation had, pre-liquidation. That's why, when Dembélé signed up at Celtic Park, we were subjected to the views of legendary coach and gesture-maker, Barry Ferguson that he was wasn't worried because 'Rangers are building a great squad.' This was wishful thinking passing for punditry.

We also had the king of the bottom-feeders, Keith Jackson, opining that Brendan Rodgers needed to shape up due to the 'credible' challenge from his former gopher Warburton.

Jackson has an even more strained relationship with credibility than he does with Celtic, who had excluded him from Paradise due to the damage he was wreaking with his crayons (quickly labelled 'the Fandan Ban'). Jackson's knowledge of the game and his command of the English language are so limited he thinks A Thesaurus plays in defence with Panathinaikos.

He is far from alone. Large swathes of the Scottish sporting media tipped Warburton's team to win the league. When Scott Brown said he expected Aberdeen to be the club's main challengers he was roundly mocked by a media pack little more than succulent lambs to the Level 5 PR slaughterhouse. Fortunately, titles and cups aren't won on back pages or websites.

Celtic's pre-season got underway on 30th June with a 2-2 draw against NK Celje. It was Tom Rogic who scored the equaliser 15 minutes from time, using his trademark shuffle to break into the box and finish with a delightful chip. Three days later it was across the border to Austria where Sturm Graz were defeated by a Ryan Christie goal.

A double from Leigh Griffiths saw Celtic beat Olimpija Ljubljana 2-1 back in Slovenia with his new striking rival Dembélé making a debut appearance. The pre-season tour ended with a 0-0 draw against Maribor who had knocked us out of the Champions League qualifiers back in Ronny Deila's first season.

It had been an experimental tour and a number of the players who took the field – Jenko, Christie, Ambrose, Allan and Henderson – would be used sparingly, if at all, in the competitive season ahead. Three days after Maribor and the first of a sequence of vital games that would shape their season was facing the Celtic squad: it was time to head for Gibraltar and the qualifying rounds of the Champions League.

Victoria Stadium in Gibraltar and Glasgow's Hampden Park are separated by 1,893 miles. Celtic's season would start at the former and finish in Scotland's national stadium. The fortunes experienced by those with Celtic in their hearts on these two occasions contrasted wildly.

Celtic took to the field on 12th July in the curious surroundings of Gibraltar, an outdated British colony (although thankfully free of Orangemen and the odd 'Sash bash'). Lincoln Red Imps were the opponents. The first time I heard the name I thought it was an American college basketball outfit. Little did we know that they would provide a blot on an otherwise excellent first year report card for our new manager.

The Celtic eleven selected (Gordon, Tierney, Janko, Ambrose, Sviatchenko, Brown, Bitton, Rogic, Christie, Griffiths and Dembélé) should have been more than enough to overcome a semi-professional side who had only played four previous ties in European competition. Yet they struggled to adapt to the artificial pitch (on which all eight teams that make up the Gibraltar Premier Division play).

Celtic in Gibraltar: between a rock and a hard place

A Dembélé 'goal' was ruled out for a foul on the keeper in the first half but Celtic were largely dominant. Then, three minutes after the interval, Lee Casciaro chased a high ball and, leaving Ambrose floundering, slipped the ball past Gordon. It was head-in-hands time for the three hundred Celtic fans who had made the journey.

There was still plenty of time to repair the damage but, despite two efforts from Griffiths coming off the crossbar, Celtic were left rueing one of their worst defeats in Europe. The Scottish press was wetting itself in excitement in the race to produce the most sensationalist headline - 'Shock of Gibraltar' proving the predictable winner.

Brendan Rodgers resisted media pressure to panic and admit the result was an embarrassment. He argued that *"one bounce caught us out"* and was confident his team would win the return tie. He undoubtedly had some sharper words for his players in private.

20 JULY: CELTIC 3 LINCOLN RED IMPS 0 ♛

Although a European game, this match saw the League flag unfurled by Tommy Burns' wife, Rosemary and Lisbon Lion, Bobby Lennox. A huge crowd of 55,632 cheered Celtic's 6th league flag in succession, but there was important business to attend to. The defeat in Gibraltar had been a sore one and a large Celtic support expected swift retribution. The new standing section was in full voice and the Green Brigade marked the occasion by unveiling a superb Spirit of the Jungle display, with an old supporter and a modern fan coming together under a Celtic OK banner.

With Patrick Roberts in the starting eleven, Celtic looked in the mood from the off. In the 22nd minute we took the lead with a fantastic shot on the turn from Mikael Lustig. 6 minutes later, Griffiths was sent clear by Roberts and, barely looking up from the edge of the penalty box, he fired a left-foot shot into the net, leaving keeper Raúl Navas no chance. Just another 4 minutes had passed when Roberts went on a dazzling run down the right wing. He beat one defender then another before playing a 1-2 with McGregor and despatching the return ball expertly past the keeper.

'Celtic OK' – North Curve display v Lincoln Red Imps

With Patrick Roberts in the starting eleven, Celtic looked in the mood from the off. In the 22nd minute we took the lead with a fantastic shot on the turn from Mikael Lustig. 6 minutes later, Griffiths was sent clear by Roberts and, barely looking up from the edge of the penalty box, he fired a left-foot shot into the net, leaving keeper Raúl Navas no chance. Just another 4 minutes had passed when Roberts went on a dazzling run down the right wing. He beat one defender then another before playing a 1-2 with McGregor and despatching the return ball expertly past the keeper. Celtic were 3-0 up in the first half hour. There was no way back for the Gibraltarians with Navas ensuring that the margin wasn't increased in the second half.

Job done. The reward was a difficult trip to Kazakhstan and the Astana Arena. Celtic had lost 2-0 there to FC Shakhter Karagandy 3 years earlier. In the post-match conference after the Lincoln game, Brendan responded to a media suggestion that it was an 'easy' draw with a heavy dose of sarcasm: *"It's a six-hour flight, five-hour time difference, 35 degrees centigrade, a plastic pitch with no water, but apart from that..."*

It was time for another friendly on Saturday 23rd July. Celtic had again been invited to play in the marketing man's wet dream of the International Champions Cup (ICC). The tournament failed to ignite the interest of many fans. The game saw the unlikely English champions, Leicester City, visit Celtic Park and win on penalties after a 1-1 draw before 25,000 fans. The top tier wasn't even open.

No thanks.

Two days later, accomplished international defender, Kolo Toure joined from Liverpool to help with Celtic's shortage of fit central defenders. Media rumours persisted that Brendan was still in the hunt for another of his former players, Scott Sinclair of Aston Villa.

27 JULY: ASTANA 1 CELTIC 1

A couple of hundred Celtic fans made the near 6000-mile round trip to the Kazakh capital for this crucial qualifying tie. Arriving to find a 3-man Celtic defence of O'Connell, Ambrose and Lustig would not have helped lift any lingering travel sickness.

It was the 20-year-old O'Connell, making his European debut, who was left floundering 19 minutes in as Astana took the lead from a corner, with Gordon left exposed in goal. This was an all-too-familiar scenario away in Europe. Gordon was forced into a superb safe following an Ambrose mistake, but that wobble aside, the makeshift defence stood strong after conceding the goal and it remained 1-0 until half-time.

In the second half, in an indication of things to come during the season, Brendan changed the team's formation. Bitton replaced Dembélé and the team went 4-5-1 in an attempt to gain more possession and slow the Astana attacks. As a result, Celtic gained a foothold in the game.

12 minutes from the end, Patrick Roberts harried a defender on the bye-line in pursuit of a lost cause. He managed to win the ball and played it back to the edge of the box where Leigh Griffiths met it beautifully with a left-foot smash. An away goal! The man known as Sparky celebrated with a kung-fu kick on a corner flag.

Two more chances came Astana's way. One was saved by Gordon and the other was incredibly headed over the bar when easier to score (anyone know the Kazakh for *Sebo*?).

A draw had been secured with a potentially vital away goal. We could get used to this.

The players greet the supporters after the draw in the Astana Arena

Two days later, a Celtic hero of a different kind went on trial at the High Court in Glasgow. The Motherwell billionaire (© Keith Jackson) known as Craigy Craigy Whyte was charged with fraud in respect of his takeover of oldco Rangers. One Gullibilly said online that the man who destroyed his club should get what he deserves *'for making hundreds of thousands of people suffer'*. A Celtic fan responded: *'Quite right – give him a knighthood!'*

It was all off to Dublin in the green on the 30th July for the next ICC game, this time against the mighty Barcelona. The Catalan Kings ran out 3-1 winners in front of an impressive crowd of over 47,000 in the Aviva Stadium but for many of the Celtic fans present the sight of Efe Ambrose marking Lionel Messi had a near laxative effect, as did the ticket price of 60 euros. Gulp!

An Efe own goal led to some Celtic fans booing the big Nigerian. That kind of treatment of your own player can never be excused, yet there were few among us who hadn't lost faith in Efe's defensive abilities a long time ago. There was no public criticism from the manager but it was to prove Efe's last meaningful appearance for the first team.

It had been an interesting and impressive first month of competitive football under Brendan Rodgers. He was busy sorting out the wheat from the chaff in the playing squad, he'd managed to navigate some difficult moments already in Europe and had experienced the 'joys' of dealing with the Laptop Loyal.

Back in his true home, in County Antrim, he would always enjoy a much more favourable reception from the local media...

CHAPTER 2 — AUGUST
It's beautiful, it's magical

OH SCOTTY SINCLAIR
HE IS SO WONDERFUL
WHEN HE SCORES A GOAL
OH IT'S BEAUTIFUL, IT'S MAGICAL

WHEN HE RUNS DOWN THE WING
HE'S AS FAST AS LIGHTNING
IT'S FRIGHTENING
AND IT MAKES ALL THE BHOYS SING...

In August 2016 Celtic signed a player whose career was in the mire. Moving to Scotland was a huge gamble for him. He had lost confidence. Others had lost faith in him. One who hadn't was Brendan Rodgers. The Irishman pulled out all the stops. He broke a family holiday in Majorca to track down his man and persuade him to follow him to Glasgow. Having worked with him before at Chelsea and Swansea City, the manager knew he was crucial to implementing the style of football he wanted his Celtic side to adopt. If he was right, it could prove beautiful. Magical even.

Yet Scott Sinclair was still an Aston Villa player. The rumours of a deal had rumbled through the summer into August and still Rodgers persisted in his attempts to bring Sinclair to Glasgow. Of greater urgency though was the impending visit to Kazakhstan in the Champions League qualifiers.

23 AUGUST: CELTIC 2 ASTANA 1

We went into this game still missing the preferred central defensive duo of Simunovic and Sviatchenko. Eoghan O'Connell was again selected in a back four with Janko, Lustig and Tierney. Celtic relied upon Roberts and Forrest on either wing to supply Griffiths who was alone up front. Astana packed out their defence and were proving impenetrable. Things were looking grim when Roberts had to be subbed on the half-hour mark due to injury (the rarely-spotted Stefan Johansen replacing him).

As the interval loomed Celtic applied more and more pressure. Armstrong and Griffiths were denied and then, just before the half ended, Tierney pursued a ball into their box and was met with a high, desperate kick in the stomach. Penalty! The Kazakhs were furious and had two players booked in protest. Despite his travails from the penalty spot last season, Leigh Griffiths stepped forward and coolly dispatched the ball home.

Things were motoring along nicely in the second half. Griffiths came close twice. A second goal would have made it comfortable for Celtic, with the away goal to fall back on.

There was a warning when Gordon was beaten by a header but it was ruled offside as the Astana players celebrated. Kolo Toure made his Celtic debut in the 60th minute as Brendan decided to shake things up at the back. He could do nothing a minute later when Gordon rushed out of his box and headed the ball clear, leaving himself stranded. Ibraimi beat Scott Brown to the loose ball and lofted it expertly over the head of Gordon and into the net despite Tierney's best efforts to stop it. Now they had an away goal and Celtic Park was silenced, other than the corner of the Main Stand hosting a small group of Astana fans.

Ten minutes later and Astana almost went 2-1 ahead. I had that horrible sinking feeling normally associated with watching Celtic in Europe under Ronny Deila at this time of the year. In contrast to the Norwegian who seemed reluctant (or unable) to change tactics and formations during a game, Brendan Rodgers would regularly shake things up to try and change the direction of a game in Celtic's favour. Fifteen minutes from the end he replaced Forrest with Dembélé. The young Frenchman had yet to score or dislodge Griffiths in the starting line-up. He had something to prove.

The 90 minutes were up. There were three minutes of injury time – with extra time looming large. I didn't fancy our chances much then. Dembélé hassled the left-back. He won the ball, nutmegged another defender in the box and then, after a lay off from Griffiths, evaded another opponent with some delightful footwork only to be cleaned out by (the delightfully named) Shitov. *'Penalty!'* screamed Celtic Park – and the referee agreed! Two Celtic penalties in one game?!? Hugh Dallas must have thrown his referees' training manual through the office window at UEFA HQ.

Dembélé opted to take the penalty. Now, this was pressure. He had no goals to his name yet. This tie was on a knife-edge. The 20-year-old did a short run up . . . then drilled the ball into the right-hand corner of the net. Paradise burst into life! Dembélé and Griffiths raced over to the corner of the North Stand and Jock Stein Stand to celebrate with the fans there. The whole ground was jumping in delight.

He'd done it. We'd done it.

North Men, South Men, Comrades All at Celtic Park

After the last-minute defeat of Astana, Brendan Rodgers took the opportunity to urge the Celtic support to be more patient and trusting in big matches where goals are proving hard to find: *"The supporters were unbelievable for us tonight but the only thing I would say to them is I think they need to show a little bit of patience as well. I'm a Celtic supporter. I know what they want and how desperately they want it but they put the players on edge at times tonight."*

The manager explained how his tactics were designed to work and the role that the fans could have in helping achieve his objectives: *"In modern football, teams are organised so if you can't play forward and you can't play sideways then you've got to come back. But when you come back we shouldn't be on edge because we're coming back. We have to circulate the ball to get out the other side and try and provoke them to become disorganised and then hopefully score a goal. Hopefully going forward, instead of having that edginess the supporters will trust the players and trust our game model and how we work and like we seen tonight we can eventually get there."* The support had to learn to adapt to the new playing style as much as the squad.

The victory had meant there was only one hurdle left on the path to Champions League qualification and we ended up drawn against Hapoel Be'er Sheva of Israel. This time, we'd play the home leg first. Whether or not Brendan Rodgers' first season would be considered successful would, in large part, be determined by these two games.

It was time to turn to domestic matters with the SPFL Premiership getting underway (at last) on the 7th August. Tynecastle away was the first of four league games which would also see us take on St Johnstone, Aberdeen and Rangers. The SPFL Fixtures Fairy had made sure there would be no easy start to Celtic's attempt to retain the title.

The day before the Hearts game, large-scale delusion was on display at Ibrokes. Despite having only just been promoted from the Championship (at the second attempt); despite having a first team that were barely recognised by most Premiership football fans and despite having a manager who appeared to be only fluent in gobshite, they declared to all and sundry that they were 'Going for 55'. Laughingly, they meant titles and not points.

This fantasy had of course been indulged by a media desperate to appease the WATP brigade. For a number of years The Gullibillies had been tub-thumping online that 'The Rangers Are Coming.' A female Celtic fan on Twitter summed up perfectly why their challenge always failed to materialise: *"Rangers are like the burd in the relationship. We tell you we are coming, but really, it's just no' happening."*

7 AUGUST: HEARTS 1 CELTIC 2   ☗

3 hours sleep. That is all the rest that Scott Sinclair had on the night of 6th August. At long last a deal had been clinched with Aston Villa after Celtic had made 5 bids for the 27-year-old Englishman. He had journeyed north and had the medical but there had been no time to train with his new team-mates. He was in the squad but didn't expect to make the bench. He was in for a rude awakening. Hearts had done well the previous season when they returned to the Premiership after one year in the Championship. Robbie Neilson had led them to third place and Europa League qualification. They hoped to do better and push Aberdeen more this season although Rangers were in the mix too. They had enjoyed a resurgence in support which meant that the number of away fans in the Roseburn Stand was now heavily restricted. They would still be heard though.

It was a great start for Celtic when, only 8 minutes into the game, Callum McGregor ran into the Hearts' penalty area and was obstructed. The ball broke to James Forrest and he scored with a delightful curling shot. It was a fine finish and a real boost for a player who looked on his way out of Celtic before the new manager's arrival. Hearts could – and should – have equalised midway through the half when former Celtic starlet Tony Watt missed an easy header.

An equaliser did come just before half-time thanks to one of Hearts' key figures in the game – referee John Beaton. Jamie Walker dived when tackled by Tierney in the box yet there was no contact between them, as was apparent to all in the ground. Beaton seized the chance to even things up, Walker himself converting the penalty then running in front of the Celtic fans to goad them. It took all of the referee's self-restraint not to join him.

The second-half provided more cut and thrust (eleven players were booked by the game's end including 4 Celts). Scott Sinclair made an unexpected debut appearance on 61 minutes. Ten minutes later, with the score still tied, Brendan withdrew O'Connell and the defence converted to a back three. He was going for it. On the 80th minute a Hearts corner was cleared to Sinclair who knocked the ball into the path of Griffiths. He went into turbo mode, haring down the left wing and leaving two Jambo defenders trailing in his wake before hitting a superb cross into their penalty box – where Sinclair arrived, having run all the way from the edge of Celtic's box, to sweep the ball past Hamilton in goal. He then raced around the net and ran along the front of the Roseburn Stand before launching himself into dozens of outstretched arms: the Celtic support were embracing a new hero.

The game was won 2-1. This seemed a different Celtic team from last season: it had backbone.

Perhaps one reason for this was Scott Brown's performance. He was back to his combative best, no longer looking jaded, and revelled in another battle at Tynecastle, one of his favourite stomping grounds. It is often suggested (especially in the media) that the Celtic captain gets away with far too much by referees.

Many media-types slavishly state this view without any evidence. During this game, the former Hearts player Allan Preston repeated the mantra on Radio Scotland: *"A lot of people believe that no matter what Scott Brown does, he won't get booked."* Less than three minutes after that comment Brown was yellow-carded. The radio silence was deafening.

The Laptop Loyal were on the crest of a wave. Not only were their beloved Bears in Scotland's top division, the signing of Joey Barton had them salivating like Andy Goram at China Buffet King. The BBC's Richard Wilson had a minute-by-minute account of Barton's league debut against Hamilton Accies, as if Messi himself had decided to end his career at the decaying Crumbledome. Curiously, the account made no mention of Barton being gloriously nutmegged by Ali Crawford (again, not part of the media's narrative) and there was little analysis of the loudmouthed Scouser's role in a drab 1-1 draw. Instead the Lapdog Loyal gleefully reported Barton's claims that no-one in the Scottish game would be able to live with him, and certainly not the Celtic captain: *"People keep talking about Joey Barton v Scott Brown. He's not even in my league – he's nowhere near the level of player I am."* That breath-taking arrogance, a trait of many associated with the Deady Bears, would be put to the test soon enough.

10 AUGUST: CELTIC 5 MOTHERWELL 0 ♘

Celtic's League Cup campaign got underway with a home tie against Mark McGhee's Motherwell. The Celtic support had been boosted before this Wednesday night game by the news that Tom Rogic had signed a new three-year deal. The new manager was moving quickly to secure those players who had impressed him in his early months at the club.

The popular Aussie celebrated the new contract in style. The game was twenty minutes old when a beautifully chipped pass from McGregor found him in the Motherwell box. He collected the ball with his right foot then slammed it home with a left-foot volley. Oooft! It was a gorgeous goal and something we were used to from the Wizard of Oz. Three more years of this stuff would do very nicely.

Scott Sinclair was patrolling the left wing for the first time at Celtic Park. Even with a five-man defence, Motherwell struggled to contain Sinclair and Rogic. The Englishman was brought down in the penalty box by Tait and Dembélé scored the resulting penalty, his second in successive home games.

Early in the second half, Rogic fed Sinclair out on the wing. He beat a defender before bending the ball around Samson for a lovely right-foot finish to open his home goals account. We could see already that there was something a bit special about this bhoy. The sight of Scott Sinclair cutting in from the wing and taking on defenders before scoring sublimely would be a feast for Celtic eyes this season. Dembélé and Rogic grabbed another goal apiece to make it 5-0 and finish off a stylish performance under the floodlights.

Celtic returned to Ireland for the final ICC game on 13th August, this time against Inter Milan in the unlikely setting of Thomond Park in Limerick, home to Munster's rugby team. It was a rare opportunity for Celtic fans in the south and west of the Emerald Isle to see their heroes in action. The game itself was little more than a training exercise for squad players on both sides, with Inter running out 2-0 winners.

No Pyro, No Party – getting lit in Limerick

The crowd of just under 13,000 had an opportunity to see Celtic Ultras in action, with red pyro lighting the sky over the Shannon at the game's start. The favourite old chant of 'One's Called Ronald, One's Called Frank' chant got an airing as one of the Ugly Sisters was now in charge of the Italian giants. He was to last only 85 days in the job – marginally longer than the couple of months he spent managing Crystal Palace the following season. Good old Irish hospitality later made up for what was a forgettable game in an entirely forgettable competition.

17 AUGUST: CELTIC 5 HAPOEL BE'ER SHEVA 2

This was a glorious summer evening in Glasgow and the ideal setting for a memorable game. If we could defeat the Israeli champions we would reach the Champions League group stages for the first time in 3 years. Qualification was Brendan Rodgers' key target for the season (others included scoring 100 goals, going undefeated at home, conceding fewer than 20 goals and claiming a domestic Treble of trophies).

It was the first time that Hapoel Be'er Sheva had appeared in the Champions League. They had beaten Olympiacos to reach this play-off game but they had rarely played in front of a crowd this big with Celtic Park heaving. The Celtic support was in good voice for this high-stakes match – as brilliantly illustrated by the Green Brigade in their pre-match display.

Going all in v Hapoel Be'er Sheva

The players certainly got the message as they took the lead only nine minutes in. A great pass from Griffiths over the Israeli defence sent Sinclair through only for him to be cleaned out by their keeper. It would have been a penalty but Rogic followed up to strike the ball home from the edge of the box. This was exactly the start needed to settle the nerves.

Celtic dominated. A penalty claim from Sinclair was ignored by the referee. Kolo Toure was at the heart of the defence. Five minutes before half-time he came tearing out of the back line and up through the middle of the park before passing to Sinclair. He set Forrest free down the right and his cross was bulleted home perfectly by Griffiths who had come racing in from the left. It was a wonderful goal worthy of being Celtic's 500th in all European competitions. The striker was so chuffed he ran all the way to the technical area and jumped into Brendan's arms!

Celtic weren't done with this exciting and exhausting first half. Griffiths won a free kick just to the right of the Hapoel box. He tee'd it up himself. He then bent the ball beautifully through the two-man wall into the top corner. An unstoppable shot! We were three up without reply and the night could not be going any better.

Hapoel had carried little threat in the first and had been swamped by Celtic. It was a different story when, ten minutes into the second half they pulled a goal back. It felt like little more than a consolation at the time. Two minutes later and Gordon had been beaten again: this wasn't a consolation, it was a comeback. The air was turning blue with all the cursing as it looked like we were yet again throwing away a comfortable lead in a vital European match. Flashbacks to the Malmo game two years were not helping the sense of growing unease. Two away goals had been conceded in as many minutes and qualification was now in jeopardy.

Brendan rung the changes and the next ten minutes saw the introduction of Bitton, Janko and Dembélé. Now, he really was going all in. He'd only been on the field three minutes when Dembélé headed Celtic 4-2 in front. The two-goal cushion was restored and the support roared its appreciation but those two away goals were preying on the mind still.

The action quickly moved to the other end when Gordon pulled off a wonder save from a header. Minutes later and Celtic survived a penalty claim. This was a game that had everything.

Celtic continued to attack, hoping to restore the thee goal lead they'd enjoyed at half-time. 5 minutes from time Scott Brown was set up by Forrest but his weak shot was blocked and the ball bounced high in the air. Before it landed the Celtic captain lashed it straight into the net. Celtic Park erupted in ecstasy! Broony celebrated with a sit-down Broony, his trademark celebration. The noise was off the scale! 5-2. Or as I heard from behind me *"FIVE F**KING TWO!!!"* We had done it. Losing two goals would have kicked most teams right in the gut. This team took it in their stride – and went out and grabbed two more.

It was a thrill watching the highlights later that night – there were so many of them. When the fifth goal was shown the commentator said: *"How crucial could that be in the grand scheme of things?"*. I remember scoffing slightly at this suggestion we'd have to rely on Broony's strike to get us through to the Group stages.

High Fives in the Champions League

Celtic's pairing with an Israeli team was always likely to generate controversy. Back in 2014 the club – along with St Johnstone and Dundalk – were sanctioned by UEFA because fans had flown the flag of Palestine at European games.

In that year more than 2000 Palestinian people had died as a result of Israeli military attacks. Celtic fans, and particularly those in the ultras section at Celtic Park, carried the Palestine flag as a show of solidarity with the fledgling state. Bizarrely, UEFA deem the flying of that country's flag to be a political act in breach of their disciplinary code.

When the Hapoel players took to the Celtic Park pitch there were hundreds of Palestinian flags and placards raised in protest in the North Curve, organised by the Green Brigade. The inevitable UEFA fine (which turned out to be £8619) duly followed a few weeks later. In the meantime, something remarkable happened.

Two days after the game, a post on the Huddleboard web forum headed up 'Match The Fine For Palestine' suggested that Celtic fans should raise funds to match whatever Celtic's fine would be and send the money on to benefit Palestinian people. The idea took root and within two days the Green Brigade launched a crowd-funding appeal to raise £15,00 to benefit the Medical Aid for Palestine (MAP) charity and the Lajee Centre for children in the Aida refugee camp.

The response from the Celtic support and beyond was phenomenal: in the first day almost £25,000 had been donated – and the following afternoon this had increased to over £100,000.

In January 2017 a large group of fans assembled in front of Celtic Park to watch the Director of the Lajee Centre receive a cheque for £176,000. It was remarkable that an act of protest in a Glasgow football ground could spark such world-wide generosity in support of an oppressed people.

Pride was felt at being part of a support prepared to stand up against injustice and a morally corrupt, money-hungry football body.

20 AUGUST: ST JOHNSTONE 2 CELTIC 4   Y

The following Saturday saw an away trip to Perth with the sold-out Celtic allocation, the first in a few years, reflecting the renewed interest in Brendan Rodgers' side. After some good early pressure with Kieran Tierney prominent, birthday bhoy Leigh Griffiths (26 today) got the party started just before the half-hour mark with a thumping volley. Within just fifteen minutes Celtic had gone 3-0 up – again! Scott Sinclair stroked home the second. 4 minutes later, James Forrest went on a fantastic run. He turned Paul Paton inside-out (no mean feat with a chin that size) and finished majestically with the outside of his right boot. McDiarmid Park was bouncing on two sides.

Celtic nursed their lead in the second half until the dying minutes. Then, in a bizarre re-run of the Hapoel game, 2 goals were conceded: a soft penalty and a goal by one of Scottish football's champion girners, Steven McLean. Surely a 3 goal lead wouldn't be lost? Substitute Ryan Christie made sure it wasn't when he grabbed a 4th goal in injury time to ease and the nerves and secure a decent victory over a strong St Johnstone side.

Thoughts now turned back to the Champions League and one of the most important games of the season.

23 AUGUST: HAPOEL BE'ER SHEVA 2 CELTIC 0

From the Holy Ground to the Holy Land: Celtic made their way to the Negev Desert to try and claim the much sought-after Champions League Group spot. Protecting a 5-2 lead should have been *reasonably* straightforward. It wasn't.

It was only fourteen minutes into the game when Saidy Jenko conceded a penalty. The foul was outside the box but the referee gave it regardless. Justice was done when Craig Gordon saved Radi's kick. Relief reigned – but only briefly. Within 5 minutes the Israelis had scored. The defence – still missing Simunovic and Sviatchenko – managed to hold on until half-time without conceding again.

Calamity struck three minutes after the re-start. Craig Gordon came off his line to claim a cross only for Janko to barge into him, knocking the ball out of the keeper's arms for it to be tapped over the line to make it 5-4 on aggregate. It was high farce but there was no funny side to it for us: Hapoel now only needed a single goal to win the tie. We'd gone from 'Doing the Huddle in the Champions League' to having a heart attack in it instead.

The remaining 42 minutes were long and cruel. An internet meme you occasionally see shared by Celtic fans had never been more appropriate: we were indeed 'Rattling Our Beads In the Champions League' as the team clung on in spite of near-incessant Hapoel attacks. Dembélé replaced Griffiths up front and soon created Celtic's first real chance of the game. The last 25 minutes was a hell all of its own. The pressure and the intense heat were taking their toll on the Celtic players. Some of them were sweating harder than a Rangers fan watching *Crimewatch*.

Sviatchenko came on to buttress the defence of Janko, Lustig, Toure and Tierney and together they held firm. When the whistle finally went, that Champions League place had finally been won. You could see what it meant to the manager as he pounded his fist against his chest in front of the 200 Celtic fans who'd endured the long journey to witness this memorable moment. The relief of the players was palpable also. Kieran Tierney was doing a mock-stagger in the style of Scott Brown while the captain (making a 70th European appearance to beat Billy McNeill's record) took part in a superb selfie with the jubilant Celtic fans behind him. It turned out that his late goal in the home leg had proven crucial after all. The Grand Old Team were back in the European big time.

For Brendan Rodgers it had proven *"probably the longest 90 minutes I have faced as a coach."* The admiration for his team was obvious: *"This match was purely about resilience and persistence and it was an amazing effort by the players on the back of everything they have been through before. But we have built into them a belief that if you work hard and with an intensity that will give you confidence and you give yourself a better chance of winning and when you are stuck you can dig it out. Tonight they added an extra percent to their mentality."*

The team's exhausting but ultimately exhilarating experience in the Middle East would stand them in good stead for the season ahead.

Doing the Broony in the Champions League!

It wasn't long before some in the Scottish media de-cried Celtic's achievement. Guardian writer and Hearts fan Ewan Murray bumped his gums to argue that Champions League qualification meant only good news for Celtic and not Scottish football generally. He seemed to have lost sight of the fact that the only regular income Hearts had from European football came through Celtic's endeavours.

The transfer window remained open and the next few days saw Stefan Johansen leave for Fulham while, no surprise at all, Saidy Janko went on loan to Barnsley. Christian Gamboa, an international right back with Costa Rica, joined the club from West Brom to take Janko's place in the squad.

There was much excitement online on Friday 25th August when the Champions League draw was made and Celtic were grouped with the English champions Man City, Borussia Monchengladbach and familiar foes Barcelona. Brendan Rodgers was realistic but defiant: *"There is no doubt we have earned the right to be here. I think everyone recognises it's an extremely tough group. But our aim, like always, is to have a go."*

27 AUGUST: CELTIC 4 ABERDEEN 1

Aberdeen had beaten Celtic twice in 4 league games the previous season and were likely to be our main challengers again this season. It was important to lay down a marker of the manager's intent with a strong performance off the back of an exhausting European away game. Celtic did that and more.

There was some shock news when Craig Gordon was dropped in in favour of new signing Dorus de Vries. The recent mistakes in Europe were undoubtedly a factor although the manager highlighted another reason: *"I need to have, for how we work, a goalkeeper that means when we have possession we have 11 players; that he can distribute the ball and pass it."*

Possession was the new watchword for Celtic: retain the ball, create chances, tire out the chasing opposition. And the keeper was expected to play his part.

The tone for this match was set early when Tom Rogic fired a shot off the Aberdeen crossbar. On the 13th minute Leigh Griffiths put his considerable skills on display, nutmegging Kenny McLean before smashing the ball past Joe Lewis and off the upright to give Celtic the lead. The timing was impeccable as the Celtic support were just about to start a minute's applause at that moment in memory of 13-year-old Kieran McDade, a Celtic fan from Coatbridge who had died the week before after collapsing at football training. The Celtic striker had met Kieran's parents before the game and after scoring he held up a shirt with 'RIP Kieran' and '13' on it in tribute to the football-loving boy.

Instead of capitalising on that great first goal, Celtic's defence failed to clear a ball and Adam Rooney grabbed an equaliser on the 32nd minute. An exquisite strike from Forrest as half-time beckoned put Celtic back into the driving seat. Again, it was the outside of his right boot that did the damage, from a fine Rogic pass.

The second half saw an Aberdeen team fail to make an impression on a tiring Celtic eleven. 3 minutes from time, Sinclair drove into the heart of the Aberdeen box between Logan and Reynolds before the ex-Motherwell man brought him down. It was a second bookable offence and earned him a red card. Sinclair sent the keeper the wrong way from the spot.

Sinclair was again involved when, in the dying seconds, he dummied a run at a free-kick to make way for Rogic to bend the ball past the wall and into the net from 30 yards out: a fitting winner for a great performance against our main domestic challengers. Just as importantly, it came after a very tough sequence of games.

The 4-1 win meant Celtic had gone top of the league for the first time with maximum points from the first 3 league games. At times they had run amok in and around opposition defences and the man doing most of the running and making us sing was Scott Sinclair. He played football the Celtic way.

As Brendan knew very well, he would bring the beauty and magic when it was needed the most.

Before the Aberdeen game, there was a street collection outside Celtic Park for the St Vincent de Paul Society. This helped connect the club back to its charitable foundations as it was the SVDP, working in the nearby Sacred Heart parish in Bridgeton, who collected and made the food for the Poor Children's Dinner Table run by Brother Walfrid that Celtic was created to support. Their great work carries on to this day and it was fitting to see so many Celtic fans put their hands in their pockets to support it.

Celtic and the SVDP: a connection spanning 130 years

TO PLAY FOOTBALL
THE BRENDAN RODGERS WAY

"This is different. This is family, this is blood, this is Patsy Gallacher, Jimmy Johnstone, Danny McGrain.

It's more than a job and it's more than a club. It's a way of life for people.

I want to make their days better and make them proud of their team."

— Brendan Rodgers, May 2016

Brendan Rodgers knows Celtic. Brendan Rodgers loves Celtic. Growing up in County Antrim in a Celtic-daft village, it could not be any different. The job as Celtic manager was unlike any other he'd had: *"I walked in here on my first day and getting ready to train, I stood and stared at my kit with the Celtic badge. It didn't feel like work anymore. This felt like a passion and a dream. So just pulling on the kit for the first time felt like when I first put on my Celtic kit that Santa brought when I was younger."*

BALLYMENA UNITED FC

BRENDAN RODGERS

This was a Celtic manager who can still recall in detail his first ever game watching the Hoops. It was a friendly against Finn Harps in Ballybofey, County Donegal and he was aged 11.

Thirteen-hour round trips from Carnlough to Celtic Park with his cousins (and the odd diversion into Baird's Bar on the Gallowgate) cemented the early affection. Watching one of the great Celts up close helped develop an enduring love for the game as well as our club: *"There was one player for me who always found the answer and always made you so excited to support Celtic and that was Paul McStay. He was an incredible player. He could pass, he could create goals and he possessed real skill and quality. He was absolutely phenomenal for Celtic."*

The style of The Maestro and Celtic's traditional attacking play helped shape the Rodgers' approach to the game. Yet there were other key early influences: *"It goes back to my life as a young man. My father loved European football; he also loved the Brazilian team. His own dad loved the Brazilian team. So I grew up loving the technical game."*

The elation that Celtic fans felt when the Carnlough man was appointed manager was not simply because he was 'Celtic-minded' which was well-known. It was also because he was a top-class coach with a shimmering reputation for fast, attacking football. Many of us felt the club wouldn't be able to entice a coach of his calibre to Scotland. His path to Celtic Park reveals much about the man but also about his management methods which had such a devastating impact in his first season in Scotland.

'I TRAVELLED ON THE BUS ONCE'

While studying at St Patrick's College in Ballymena, a 32-mile round journey from Carnlough, the young Rodgers started playing team football regularly. He became an accomplished youth player with the successful Star United who were based in Ballymena (he used to wear his Hoops to their training sessions) and as a teenager made it into the reserve team of the town's Irish League side. His father Malachy used to take him to training or games and if he couldn't make it Brendan would make do with the bus. With a clever left-foot he could play in either midfield or defence. He was selected for Northern Ireland Schools on seven occasions and had a trial with Man United in 1988. One of his Star United playing colleagues remembers him as *"more of a young Tommy Burns than an Owen Archdeacon. He didn't have great pace, but had a lovely first touch, good vision, good passer, great crosser of a ball. A proper footballer."*

Brendan as a youth player (third from left, front row)

In 1991, at 18, he moved across the Irish Sea to join Reading as an apprentice. Within two years his playing career was finished due to a persistent knee injury. His dream of making it as a professional footballer was over. *"I never made the first team, although I travelled on the bus once."* He wasn't heading back to Ireland though.

His experience of the playing side had stoked his desire to stay involved in the game: *"I played in teams that were not technical. So I spent more time without the ball than with it. I always wanted to change that. So my ideology was: "OK, I'm not going to have an influence on the game as a player, technically or tactically. Can I do it as a coach?" My objective was to show that British players could play football. That was the challenge."*

It meant starting at the bottom rung. He already had commitments: he was married with children. Yet the challenge was to prove his making. He worked 12 hour shifts, five days a week, in a warehouse in Bracknell while doing his coaching badges in the evenings. The inspiration came from his hard-working parents who had brought up five children and emphasised to them that great things could be achieved through dedication and effort.

With his coaching qualifications in the bag, he was offered a full-time job with Reading as Under-11s coach and Welfare Officer. He ended up in overall charge of the youth set-up with the Royals. His commitment to self-improvement continued – he travelled in the Netherlands and Spain studying youth academies.

Reading ranks – before injury struck

He saw value in a club having a single philosophy of football which was imbued in players in the youth teams and reached fulfilment in the first team. He developed contacts at Barcelona, Valencia and Sevilla, learning Spanish along the way. The next step in his career progression came about thanks to a Portuguese national whom Celtic fans were already very familiar with.

In September 2004, aged 31, Brendan's Reading team comfortably beat Chelsea's youths at Stamford Bridge. The new Chelsea manager, Jose Mourinho, was so impressed that he offered to put Rodgers in charge of youth development at the West London club. He didn't have to ask twice: *"They wanted to put his tactical ideas in practice throughout the club – his two favourite systems were the 4-4-2 diamond and the 4-3-3 – and I was one of the few British coaches who walked that way. We connected straight away."*

Over the new few years Chelsea dominated the English game and Brendan was promoted to Reserve Team Coach. The experience had been challenging yet rewarding and had set him up nicely to branch out: *"By the time I finished at Chelsea I had 15 years working as a coach from five-year-olds to the Ballacks, the Decos, the Shevchenkos, the Lampards. Then it was my time to walk alone. You cannot take man-management from Mourinho: it has to be from you."*

YOU'LL NEVER SEE A PIANIST RUN AROUND HIS PIANO

His first manager's job came when he took charge of Championship side Watford in November 2008. The team were in the relegation zone and things did not improve after only two wins in the next 10 games. He managed to guide them out of the danger zone and enjoyed an FA Cup run to the 5th round. It had been a successful start but in the close season Reading manager Steve Coppell resigned and Brendan was tempted back to the familiar environs of the Madejski Stadium. It proved a disastrous return: he was sacked within six months as the club languished in a relegation spot. It was another harsh lesson that football had taught him.

After six months out of work, Brendan replaced Paolo Sousa as manager of Swansea City, another Championship club, in July 2010. Having made it to seventh spot in the league the season before, Swansea progressed to third place under the new manager and entered the play-offs. There they beat Nottingham Forest before, as luck would have it, facing Reading in the final. It must have been sweet to watch his new team beat the club who had sacked him by 4-2 – thanks to a Scott Sinclair hat-trick.

They were the first Welsh team to be promoted to the EPL. The Rodgers' stock was rising again.

In the top division, Swansea didn't just make up the numbers in the relegation battle as many had predicted. The football analyst Jonathan Wilson highlighted the playing style that earned the Welsh club multiple plaudits: *"Swansea played their precise, passing football, racking up possessions stats to compare with those of Barcelona or Bayern Munich. They defied expectations, not merely surviving but thriving."*

Wins over Arsenal and Liverpool were highlights of an excellent debut season in which Swansea secured 11th place, 11 points clear of the relegation berths. The results and attacking style of play attracted great praise. Possession was king, as Rodgers explained to a visiting journalist: *"We were favourites to be relegated but our biggest success has been our philosophy, our identity of football. The players have been incredible in their capacity to play our style of football . . . All players want to attack – and our way of defending is to have the ball."*

Total Football in the Welsh valleys

The Irishman went on to explain how his team played the way that he wanted them to: *"Of course, you want the players to believe and you get to this by working on it every day on the training ground, with the ball at their feet . . . By working on the field, by watching videos, everything we did on the training pitch, we did with the ball. You'll never see a pianist run around his piano."*

His sensational two seasons at Swansea meant he was now hot property. When Kenny Dalglish stepped down from the Liverpool job for a second time, it was Brendan Rodgers they turned to – attracted by the attacking football which he championed and which had long been considered a Liverpool trait. He would later describe his three and a half years in charge at Anfield as *"incredible but complicated."*

At the start of his reign he explained in a meeting with Liverpool fans why he felt possession was crucial to his management of games: *"When you've got the ball 65 to 70 per cent of the time, it's a football death for the other team. It's death by football."* That was why he immediately moved on players such as Andy Carroll, Stewart Downing and Charlie Adam at a considerable loss: he had no interest in playing with wingers and a target man. He preferred fluid formations which could be altered during the course of the game and needed players who were comfortable retaining possession rather than throwing hopeful balls forward.

His first season at Anfield saw marginal improvements. Rodgers then proved he was prepared to be fluid also, adapting his philosophy to suit the players at his disposal. As Jonathan Wilson wrote of his second season in charge: *"They played direct, raid football, using the pace of Luis Suarez, Daniel Sturridge and Raheem Stirling."* The effect was electric. An 11-game winning streak that started in February 2014 thrust them to the top of the League.

With only three games left Liverpool were five points clear of Man City and on the cusp of their first League title since 1990. A 2-0 defeat at home to Chelsea (featuring the infamous Gerrard slip) gave Man City, who had a game in hand and a far superior goal difference, advantage. Liverpool then went away to Crystal Palace and were 3-0 up after 55 minutes.

They went chasing more goals, urged on by their fans. In the last 11 minutes they conceded three goals – and two points. Man City won the title a week later by two points and a +14 goal difference. It has been an occasional criticism of Brendan Rodgers that his commitment to attacking football is too stringent and more pragmaticism is required in certain games.

The toast of the Kop – before it all went sour

The following season Liverpool sold Suarez and brought in Balotelli and Ricky Lambert and finished 6th in the League. They failed to make an impact in Europe and defensively they remained frail. While it was rumoured that a 'transfer committee' rather than the manager alone was responsible for signings, he had ultimately failed to improve the fortunes of the Anfield club or win a trophy. Early into his fourth season in charge, he was sacked to make way for Jurgen Klopp as his team sat in eleventh place in the EPL.

The Liverpool experience must have been life-changing for Rodgers. He was managing a globally-recognised club, he'd been subjected to major scrutiny from the tabloid press for the first time and he came within a whisker of winning the EPL in only his third season managing at that level.

It ultimately ended on a sour note though: only a few months before his sacking he had signed a new four-year contract and had been given assurances he would be in charge at Liverpool for the foreseeable future. It was not to be.

YOU HAVE HEARD US CALLING IN THE NIGHT

Rodgers didn't rush back into another job. He took time out, enjoying his first proper break in over 6-and-a-half years, and an opportunity to take stock on what had been a rollercoaster ride in the upper echelons of football management. He thought carefully about where he wanted to go next.

It was a meeting with Dermot Desmond and Peter Lawwell at the Irish billionaire's London home that proved the turning point. The three men got on well straight away. The experience of managing Celtic, a club he knew from his earliest days, would be very different from the jobs he'd had. Champions League football was a possibility and he was the man most likely to guide Celtic into the group stages. There was also the lure of silverware. And one particular historic record to beat that could turn him into a true legendary figure in Celtic folklore...

In his first season as Celtic manager it was clear that he introduced a level of professionalism that hadn't been seen for some years. The relentless, unbeaten domestic run demonstrated that he had brought a focus and determination into a first team that had lost its way. It is incredible to think that in his first 12 months in the job he surpassed Martin O'Neill's treble-winning year of 2000-2001.

His philosophy of attacking football based on possession and the 'counter-press' remain unchanged. He is clear in what his aim is at Celtic: *"We're trying to build a consistent Champions League club here so you have to have a Champions League mentality."*

One example of that is the targets he set his team in their first season together. seven in all including Champions League Group qualification; a domestic treble; to go the full season undefeated at home; and to score over 100 League goals.

It is believed that all targets were met with the exception of conceding less than 20 goals in the League. The targets helped ensure that the players understood and remained focused on what the manager wanted them to achieve as the season progressed.

It was clear that he would change the team's formation during games as and when required. The need to retain possession and keep the ball on the ground led to Craig Gordon being dropped until he showed he could adapt to the new style: he did and has prospered as a result.

THIS YEAR WE'LL GIVE IT TO BRENDAN RODGERS

HOOPS BAR C.S.C

It didn't take the new manager long to win the hearts of Celtic supporters

Brendan was able to persuade many of Ronny Deila's players of the value of his different approach to the game and those who have adapted have flourished, including Stuart Armstrong, James Forrest and Dedryck Boyata. Gary Mackay-Steven was one of the few non-success stories. He helped reinvigorate the captain, Scott Brown to an extent that he had one of his most influential seasons in the Hoops. He brought in tried and trusted players (Scott Sinclair, Kolo Toure) and persuaded the great talent that is Moussa Dembélé that he and Celtic could provide a stage for him to show off his skills at the highest level of European football.

Before they ran out at Hampden for the Scottish Cup Final, when the players were on the brink of winning a Treble and securing the status of Invincibles, the manager told them: *"You have to make history – it doesn't just happen."*

They did. And he helped make it happen, for he has an acute sense of history. When, in the week he signed a new four-year contract, he was asked by the media if the 10 fingers he held up at the end of the Kilmarnock signified he was indeed "here for 10 in a row" as the chant says. Brendan responded with a knowing smile: *"I was just stretching my fingers."*

He knows. We know. Brendan Rodgers – here for 10 in a row.

Brendan – one of the (Carnlough) Bhoys

CHAPTER 3 — SEPTEMBER
It filled his heart with joy

HE DREAMT OF PLAYING FOR CELTIC
EVER SINCE HE WAS A BHOY
HE SIGNED WHEN HE WAS 7
IT FILLED HIS HEART WITH JOY

AND NOW HE'S IN THE FIRST TEAM
HIS DREAM IT HAS COME TRUE
HE'S THE BEST LEFT BACK IN SCOTLAND
AND HE'S CELTIC THROUGH AND THROUGH

The frequent international breaks in the Premiership campaign are a source of discontent for many Celtic fans. A fortnight without Celtic causes serious withdrawal symptoms. Fortunately for those Tims in and around the Fife area there has long been an alternative attraction when the international break falls in early September.

As every Celtic fan knows, Cardenden in west Fife is home to one of our club's most legendary figures: John Thomson, the Prince of Goalkeepers. Following his tragic death in 1931, John lies at rest in Bowhill Cemetery close to where he grew up. The cemetery has long been a place of pilgrimage for Celtic fans, specially around the anniversary of his death – 5th September – and whenever Celtic are playing in Fife.

In 1983 a local Celtic fan Alex Burns conceived the idea of a street football tournament for primary school kids from the 3 villages that make up Cardenden to be organised in memory of John. The event is now well established and organised on the weekend closest to the anniversary. On 4th September 2016 the Guest of Honour was a living Celtic legend, Danny McGrain, who remains one of the most popular captains in the club's history. The tournament winners were Bowhill Rovers and Danny handed out trophies to all the participants before leading a large crowd of locals and Celtic supporters to the nearby cemetery where floral tributes were laid at John Thomson's grave.

On his headstone it says *'They Never Die Who Live In The Hearts They Leave Behind.'* Every September, the community of Cardenden and the Celtic support ensure that remains true of our Darling Johnny.

John Thomson remembered in Cardenden in 2016

'They Hung Out The Flag of War' proclaims the famed rebel song about the 1916 Easter Rising, 'The Foggy Dew.' This was the declaration that greeted a sell-out Celtic Park from the new standing section as the current incarnation of Rangers visited for the first time. The whole of the North Curve was bedecked in green, white and orange ponchos creating a huge, heaving, human Irish tricolour. It was an extraordinary sight and set the tone perfectly for the battle ahead that Celtic were determined to win.

The North Curve puts out the flag of war

It was a gloriously warm and sunny day and the beachballs that were out in force to celebrate the upcoming midweek visit to Barcelona looked perfectly at home. Few of us predicted just how much fun in the sun lay ahead in the next 90 minutes.

Leigh Griffiths was out injured and it was Moussa Dembélé who led the Celtic frontline. On 33 minutes it was a fine headed goal by Dembélé from a Scott Sinclair corner that put the Bhoys ahead – and the human tricolour burst into life! 9 minutes later, Bitton intercepted a ball in midfield and his defence-splitting pass sent Dembélé through, his run being tracked by Senderos. Dembélé cut back, Senderos went sliding past him and then the young Frenchman, showing nerves of steel, hit the ball with the outside of his right foot past a despairing Foderingham to put the Celts 2-0 up. He was on a hat-trick now.

The last Celtic player to score a hat-trick against a team calling itself Rangers was Harry Hood way back in 1973. Could he be a Zombie-skelper and history-maker in the same day?

The players celebrated the goal in front of the North Curve. As Brown and Lustig were making their way through the penalty box to join the celebration, they jogged past a dejected Joey Barton – and the Swedish defender had a burst beachball on his head! It was a surreal moment in what was proving an unreal afternoon for the loudmouthed Scouser who had declared previously that the Celtic skipper wasn't in his league.

Life's a beach and then Rangers die!

In the last minute of the first half Rangers pulled a goal back through Garner, which made the gap between the teams look a lot narrower than it actually was. Would Celtic pull away after a Brendan team-talk? The outside of Moussa Dembélé's right foot had a further part to play. On the 61st minute Armstrong fed the ball to Dembélé whose pass with that favoured foot went through the middle of Kiernan and Senderos into the path of the on-running Scott Sinclair. He tucked the ball away beautifully past Foderingham. 3-1.

Celtic continued to press and a headed clearance put Senderos under pressure as he misjudged a bounce with Dembélé on his shoulder and handled the ball to prevent a certain goal.

Even Willie Collum had to accept it was a sending off and Celtic now had a man advantage. 7 minutes from the end, Lustig bombed down Celtic's right flank and chipped the ball over the Rangers defence to Dembélé who was loitering with intent at the back post.

The young Frenchman controlled the cross beautifully with his right foot and then smashed it home with his left – for the perfect hat-trick of left-foot, right foot and head! He ran towards the corner of the Main Stand and Jock Stein Stand with three of his fingers in the air. He had just written his name into the history books.

Celtic were not finished there though. Another attack was started by Kieran Tierney who passed down the wing, ran beyond for the return pass – leaving Tavernier trailing in his wake – and when the cross came in just beyond the penalty spot, there was Stuart Armstrong – who had looked impressive since coming on as a sub for Rogic in the 54th minute – to control the ball and smack it in the opposite corner. Celtic Park erupted in joy for an incredible fifth time.

One of the loudest chants throughout the game had been *"You're Not Rangers Anymore"* and for many in the Celtic support the day proved beyond doubt – despite all the media hype – that this Rangers were a shadow of their former selves. A defining image of the day was a dejected Joey Barton looking down into the Rangers net where the match ball nestled among a couple of beachballs while Celtic players in the background celebrated the 5th goal. This was humiliation and hubris on a grand scale: *"They won't be able to live with me"* had been his boast. Yet Celtic and Scott Brown destroyed his career that day. He never played again in Scotland and when he returned south later that season he was hit with a FA ban of 18 months for breaching gambling rules. The last laugh belonged to Scott Brown.

Celtic were now 4 points clear with a game in hand. This was a humiliating result all round for Rangers. Mark Warburton had built a team that had coasted the Championship but the top league was proving an altogether different proposition. The only sustained attacking in Rangers colours that day had been when their fans trashed the undefended Celtic Park toilets. Warburton was branded 'the English Paul Le Guen' after the game.

He looked tactically naive and his bizarre, mumbled public post-match statements were another stick to beat him with. An old Paul Le Guen chant came back to mind: *"Warburton's gonna get the sack – we won the league before the clocks went back."*

Celtic had made a statement. We'd played our 4 main opponents in the first 4 games of the season – and won them all. We were also 15 goals for and only 5 against in those 4 games. This season was shaping up very nicely.

13 SEPTEMBER: BARCELONA 7 CELTIC 0　　　🏆

Four days later and Celtic came back to earth with an almighty bump in Catalonia. We had craved a return to the Champions League but the draw had not been kind. Barcelona with Messi, Suarez and Neymar up front. English Champions Man City bankrolled by Arab billions. The only genuine hope of picking up points was Borussia Monchengladbach who were no mugs.

The grim reality of the financial gulf between Celtic and the Champions League crème-de-la-crème was laid bare this night in the Nou Camp. Messi predictably scored early but Celtic were handed a lifeline when a brilliant Sinclair run put Dembélé through who was then upended by their goalie, Tor Stegen. Dembélé took the penalty but the German saved it with ease and a golden opportunity to at least contain Barca for a while was lost. Messi and Neymar combined for the second, which meant 2-0 at half-time. If only they'd taken their foot of the gas.

Five second half goals, including great strikes from Neymar and Suarez and another for Messi to give him a hat-trick, meant this was Celtic's worst ever European result. Despite that, the reaction from the Celtic support was muted. We had held out no great hope – and our focus was on improving domestically. Any improvement at a Champions League level was always going to be gradual at best. This was a night and performance to forget – and quickly.

The beachballs were well and truly burst.

The red and blue of Barca was swapped for that of Inverness Caley Thistle in Celtic's first trip to the Highlands of the season. The Tulloch Caledonian Stadium had proven a tricky place for the Bhoys to visit since the club were first promoted to the top division back in 2004. The six-hour round journey from Glasgow at least afforded fans the opportunity for some refreshment on the way up and down.

Celtic took an early lead (yet again) in 17 minutes after Tierney rampaged down the left and sent in a ball with the outside of his left foot that Rogic finished off neatly. A superb right foot strike from Caley's Billy King beat De Vries' outstretched hand for an equaliser 10 minutes later. Celtic then survived a strong penalty claim before a surging Sinclair run followed by a beautiful bending shot around the keeper's outstretched hand restored the lead. 2-1 at half-time.

In the second half, another lung-bursting run from Tierney was followed by a blistering shot which was foiled before Callum McGregor had the crossbar shaking from an excellent strike. Keeper Fon Williams then kept out another tremendous McGregor effort before the crossbar again saved ICT, this time from a certain KT goal. Erik Sviatchenko then hit a post with a header.

The traffic was all one-way but the third goal just wasn't coming. Then, with a minute remaining, Celtic failed to clear a corner and De Vries was beaten by a header from Fisher. These were the first dropped points of the season – and it felt like all 3 had been lost given the multitude of great chances created.

One memorable footnote to this game was that Scott Sinclair's first half goal meant he was the first Celt since the great Jimmy McGrory to score in his first 5 League games.

Next up was the League Cup (officially the Betfred Cup) and a visit from Alloa Athletic, recent conquerors of Rangers and the subject of an infamous fan chant which illustrated perfectly how the 'mighty' had fallen: *"Same old Alloa, Always Cheating."* There was no such chicanery tonight from the Ochils team although the League One leaders, managed by Jack Ross, proved a very difficult nut to crack.

A sub-standard performance from Patrick Roberts saw him hooked at half-time as the solid Alloa defence proved difficult to breach. It was marshalled by Jim Goodwin, a former Celtic youth and St Mirren stalwart, who has one of those faces so common in Scottish football that you would never tire of slapping with a wet fish.

Craig Gordon was back between the sticks. He was lucky to survive a red card early in the game after a reckless tackle outside his box halted Greg Spence. Alloa offered little up front at other times.

The second half was more of the same. The Alloa goalkeeper pulled off a number of fine saves, especially from Forrest. The last 10 minutes arrived and it was still 0-0. It was a small crowd and the discontent inside Celtic Park was increasing. Would the Barcelona debacle and dropped points at Inverness be followed by a failure to beat the part-timers?

Fortunately, a devastating run from Forrest finally gave Celtic the lead in the 83rd minute. A brilliant take and turn from Dembélé on the 90th minute was followed by a direct hit into the roof of the net, his 8th goal of the season, guaranteeing safe passage into the semi-final where Rangers were waiting.

It was an uncomfortable night and after the game Brendan Rodgers heaped praise on Alloa: *"They made it very, very difficult. Big applause for them."* Celtic broke them down eventually but they'd proved harder to overcome than most Premiership teams to date.

Dorus de Vries was back between the sticks for this visit from Kilmarnock but he looked less than impressive just after the half-hour mark when Kilmarnock took a shock lead. It was a wonder strike from Souleymane Coulibaly (who would soon leave the wastelands of Ayrshire for the deserts of Egypt in a £800,000 move) that beat de Vries from 35 yards out yet, despite the quality and daring of the striker, there was a suspicion that the Dutchman's positioning was at fault. Curiously, he didn't re-appear in the second half (due to a chest problem it was reported) and Craig Gordon had the keeper's jersey again. But could he keep it?

The fear that things were not going to go our way in this game was soon curbed when two fine finishes from Dembélé within 3 minutes gave Celtic a half-time lead. Great interplay between Forrest and Rogic saw the former score seven minutes into the second half.

Leigh Griffiths returned to duty after injury in a second-half substitution for Dembélé and just 3 minutes later he was back on the scoresheet with a cheeky header. When he later won a penalty he showed some good team spirit to offer it up to Scott Sinclair, who dispatched it past Jamie MacDonald to surpass Jimmy McGrory's long-standing record. The Englishman was finding a home-from-home at Celtic Park. An error from the Killie keeper saw Tom Rogic claim Celtic's 6th goal in what was an impressive display of clinical, attacking football after an early setback.

There was a funny moment after the game when my kids asked to stay on to get some selfies and autographs with the players. When Dorus de Vries appeared my daughter had her photo taken with the keeper. He was enjoying some good-natured banter with the fans about the Coulibaly goal and explained he'd misjudged the height of the ball. I then asked my 7-year-old son if he wanted his photo taken with the new Celtic keeper. When he didn't respond I asked him again and he whispered in my ear: *"He's a loser."* This was a bit harsh. No photo was taken and whenever the Dutchman's name came up the rest of the season it was met with a frown and a shake of the head: the unforgiving nature of youth!

The 6-1 game was a memorable experience for one particular bhoy that day: Caidan Mullan had come all the way from Belfast to Paradise with the Ardoyne Youth Club. They were guests of the Kano Foundation, a unique initiative by a group of Celtic supporters that has been raising funds since 2010 to pay for whole groups of schoolkids from all over Scotland, the UK and Ireland to attend a game at Celtic Park for the first time – and for free.

Caidan Mullan – the Kano Foundation's 5000th child over the turnstile

The Foundation pays for a block of season tickets in the Lisbon Lions Stand each year then arranges for groups from schools, community and youth centres to travel to Glasgow where they get fed before entering Celtic Park and cheering on The Bhoys. Caidan was significant as he was the 5000th child that the Kano Foundation had brought 'over the turnstile' into Paradise.

The Kano Foundation is entirely dependent upon donations from the Celtic support and their annual bucket collection at Celtic Park is vital to them Keeping Football Free For Kids. They are a credit to the club and support and have ensured that thousands of kids have experienced the joy (and occasional sorrow!) of seeing Celtic in action in Paradise. Hopefully their great work will continue for years to come.

There was much gnashing of teeth the following day when Aberdeen played Rangers for the first time in 5 years at Pittodrie. The Dons won the game in the final minute from a disputed free-kick. Mark Warburton was raging at the referee in a most undignified manner on the pitch. This is not how he had been led to believe referees generally behaved when giving the honour taking charge of a game involving The Rangers. Much sadness prevailed.

28 SEPTEMBER: CELTIC 3 MAN CITY 3

What an incredible night this was. Celtic fought the English Champions toe-to-toe and to a virtual standstill. Man City had won all 10 of their previous games in a blistering start to the season. The noise and atmosphere were exceptional as the excitement levels cranked up with each goal. Brendan Rodgers said in the post-match conference that it was *"a noise I've never heard before."* Welcome to Paradise on a Champions League night.

The Green Brigade display in the North Curve featured a line from a modern Celtic song that neatly summarised the support's feelings about the kind of football the team were playing under the new manager – and the hope we could bring it to the Champions League: *'It's such a joy for us to see, for they play football the Celtic way.'*

The Joy of Celtic: Man City's trip to Paradise

Only 3 minutes had passed when Celtic took the lead. A Sinclair free kick was clipped into the goalmouth by Forrest and Sviatchenko's header glanced off Dembélé's chest and past Bravo to cause an explosion of noise around Celtic Park. Seven minutes later, a lucky break of the ball saw Fernandinho claim an equaliser while the Celtic defence shouted for offside – to no avail. The wind hadn't been taken out of the Celtic sails though. A magnificent through ball from Rogic set up Tierney whose first-time cross was deflected by Raheem Stirling into his own net. In the lead again – and still only 20 minutes on the clock! As the young Motherwell bhoy ran towards the fans his face matched ours: disbelief and utter, unconfined joy. We all knew how good he was. Here he was letting everyone in the Champions League know.

Within no time at all the stadium was rocking to *Sha-La-La-La-La-La-La! Kie-ran Tierney!*

Within ten minutes it was KT's turn to track a run from Stirling after he'd been fed a great ball by David Silva. A great turn from the English internationalist was followed by a fine conversion. It was all square again.

Just two minutes after the re-start and Celtic fans were again enjoying the brilliance of Moussa Dembélé. The Man City defence failed to deal with a Tierney cross and it found its way to Dembélé, in space in the penalty box with his back to goal. He controlled it with his knee – then spectacularly hit it past Bravo with an overhead kick! It was a sensational finish from a player whose goals were making him a darling of the Celtic support. There was a long way to go though and City came out fighting after their third reverse. Within ten minutes of Celtic's goal – again! – City equalised. This time Craig Gordon was unlucky to see a very good save from Aguerro fall into the path of Nolito. 3-3.

There was more than half an hour to go in this incredible encounter. Increasingly, City dominated.

A brilliant one-handed save from Gordon stopped Gundogan from stealing all 3 points on the night. Celtic saw the game out through sheer grit and determination and nerves were well and truly shredded by the time the final whistle blew. Kolo Toure had been an absolute leader in our defence: imperious, commanding and unflappable. Scott Brown demonstrated that he still had so much to offer at this level. It was a true captain's performance from him.

The London-based Independent newspaper captured the spirit of what had been an uplifting and exhausting night under the lights in Paradise: *'There was an extraordinary moment, as the Champions League's anthem sounded, when Celtic Park burst into a long and monumental roar of expectation and you saw what the grand European stage means to this place. Few British stadiums can create such a noise and the Celtic players were drenched in its spirit, as the rain drifted across the place, carried on the wind whipping up from across Glasgow's East End. The noise persisted to the end as Celtic threw themselves into blocks and challenges.'*

THIS is what we had been missing so much: going up against a top outfit and matching them for long periods. It was an important step in trying to restore Celtic's European reputation.

It felt like the club had taken an important step forward – and there, seemingly at the heart of everything, was Kieran Tierney.

One of our own who no longer just represented the future: this former ball boy had shown he could do more than just compete among the elite of European football.

The future is here.

CHAPTER 4 — OCTOBER
Let this moment linger

GRACE JUST HOLD ME IN YOUR ARMS

AND LET THIS MOMENT LINGER

THEY'LL TAKE ME OUT AT DAWN

AND I WILL DIE

WITH ALL MY LOVE

I PLACE THIS WEDDING RING

UPON YOUR FINGER

THERE WON'T BE TIME TO SHARE OUR LOVE

SO WE MUST SAY 'GOODBYE'

1 OCTOBER: DUNDEE 0 CELTIC 1 ⚐

October kicked off with a visit to Dens Park to face ex-Celt Paul Hartley's team who were struggling near the foot of the table. After the exertions of the Man City game, it wasn't surprising that Celtic were sluggish up front. Although carrying little attacking threat themselves, Dundee were dogged in defence and half-time came without a Celtic goal being scored in the opening 45 minutes – for the first time in the League this season.

Any creeping concerns were soon banished when Scott Brown proved match-winner just two minutes after the break. The captain had followed up on a move he'd started, hitting a decent left-foot shoot through a melee of players into the net. The introduction of Griffiths and Roberts didn't result in any more goals but the win was secure. Yet again Rodgers' men had shown they were capable of getting a result after a tough Champions League encounter. The single-goal win meant Celtic retained top spot in the League going into yet another international break. Booooooooooooo!

15 OCTOBER: CELTIC 2 MOTHERWELL 0 ⚐

Motherwell were keen to demonstrate that they'd tightened up since their visit back in August when they'd shipped five goals. They appeared happy to sacrifice space on the wing to protect the middle in order to stifle Celtic. Their plan became unstuck when a great James Forrest in the 18th minute run sliced open their defence. His pass was slotted home with ease by Scotty Sinclair (after Dembélé hit fresh air with his original attempt).

Yet Celtic struggled to build on that lead. Motherwell keeper Craig Sampson kept them in the game with some fine saves. He didn't stop a superb effort from Kieran Tierney which had the fans up on their feet in acclamation – but the crossbar did. KT featured in another excellent cameo. In one extended run all the way down the left wing he managed to beat 3 Well players (almost skinning one of them with an incredible turn) and firing a shot which went narrowly over. Not for the first time the young Celt had the crowd chanting his name in admiration.

The game remained too close for comfort until the death when Dembélé chased a forlorn ball and managed to win a penalty – which he converted with aplomb. He earned the praise of the manager post-match: *"That looked like it was dead and was going to go through to the keeper but he made it something. The best strikers do that and create something out of nothing or make something for themselves. He made the penalty through his endeavour."*

It was another three points in the bag however more than just endeavour would be needed with Borussia Monchengladbach next up at Celtic Park.

19 OCTOBER: CELTIC 0 BORUSSIA MONCHENGLADBACH 2 🏆

It had bruised the considerable ego of The Rangers' support in recent years when the slogan 'Glasgow's Green and White' had taken hold while they were polluting Scottish football's lower reaches.

Cue much online bleating and sash-slashing when photos emerged of a free Celtic Family Zone being hosted in George Square on the day the Bundesliga team came to Glasgow. The perma-raging were frothing at the mouths again with their paranoid claims of a conspiracy involving Celtic, the Vatican and Glasgow City Council.

Our German visitors were welcomed with open arms. Celtic fans have long enjoyed trips to Germany where there is a thriving football culture and a seemingly endless supply of beer. Borussia's fans certainly got into the spirit of things on this visit to Glasgow. Before the game, as large numbers of them were walking past The Celtic Way on London Road, one started singing 'The Huns are going bust – again!' to great acclaim. His afternoon in the Gallowgate had not been educational as well as enjoyable.

When the Group draw was made it had wrongly been assumed by some that with Celtic unlikely to take much from either Barca or Man City, beating the Germans was our only realistic gateway to third place and a drop into the Europa League. No-one told Borussia that was how it was meant to be.

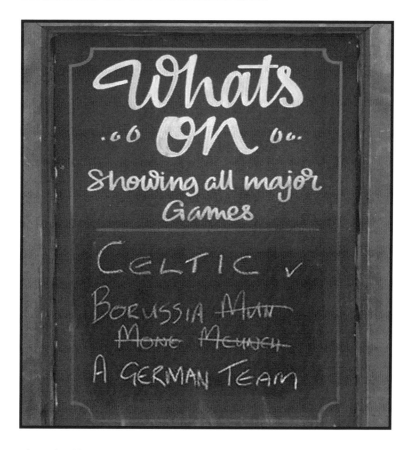

There had been a lot of mirth in the build up to this game when an Edinburgh pub had advertised the match on a board where they gave up on attempting to spell the lengthy name of Celtic's German opponents. A photo of the sign went viral in UK and Germany. Borussia responded by re-naming themselves 'A German Team' on Twitter and even produced scarves with the label also.

The laughter dried up not long after the game got underway when it became apparent that these Germans were no innocents abroad. Even though they were missing two key players – Hazard and Raffael – through injury, BMG controlled the first half, created chances and kept the Celtic support largely quiet throughout. This was in stark contrast to the Man City game. Craig Gordon was called into action time and again. There was no let-up from the Germans and it was blessed relief when the half-time whistle went.

This opportunity to re-group was much needed but it only proved a short break from the onslaught. Just after ten minutes into the second half Kolo Toure tried to shepherd a ball out to safety – only to lose possession on the line and for Stindl to smack the ball home through Gordon's legs. Still Celtic struggled to get a foothold in the game and twenty minutes later it was all over after Toure gifted possession and was punished mercilessly by Andre Hahn. He was at least brave enough to face up to the media afterwards: *"In that kind of competition, you can't afford to make those kind of mistakes. I have to blame myself. Even though I'm 35 years old, I'm still making 16-year-old mistakes."*

It was a night to forget for the popular Ivorian defender and the Celtic support. It was a good thing for us that the next game was against some Scottish minnows...

23 OCTOBER: RANGERS 0 CELTIC 1   ♟

It was a wet Hampden afternoon as Celtic met a Rangers team led by Mark Warburtorn still labouring under the illusion it could challenge Celtic on various fronts. This was another opportunity to bring them crashing back to earth.

Memories of the recent 'Dembelition' were evoked with balloons featuring the Frenchman celebrating his historic hat-trick and the line 'You're Not Rangers Any More.'

Some of the balloons had even made it as far as Brendan's home-town across the Irish Sea.

An early Tom Rogic effort almost looped over goalkeeper Gilks to give the Celts an early lead. Our hearts were in our mouths a short while later though when it looked as though Craig Thomson awarded Rangers a penalty and ended up booking McKay for a blatant dive. Smelling salts had to be passed around the Celtic players at an honest decision – rather than mistake - from the Paisley referee. Celtic then piled on the pressure. Gilks saved well from Sinclair and then almost gifted Rogic the easiest of goals before recovering just in time.

After the break it looked as though Celtic had finally taken the lead when Sviatchenko smartly headed a Sinclair cross home – only for Thomson to rule it out for an imaginary foul on Clint Hill. Gilks again denied Sinclair and then it was the crossbar's turn to defy after an excellent Sinclair free-kick. Celtic enjoyed almost all the possession and pressure – it had taken 50 minutes for Warbiola's men to finally get a shot on target. At one point Scott Brown launched a fantastic scissor challenge on Andy Halliday that had the Deady Bears' captain clutching the ball like a pillow while pleading asylum from the ref. Yet doubts started to grow among the Celtic fans as the ball steadfastly refused to cross their line. It was thanks to Simunovic that a shot from Holt didn't give them the lead on the hour mark.

Nerves were beginning to jangle in spite of Celtic's domination.

Twenty minutes from the end Brendan decided to go with two up front, bringing on Griffiths for Rogic. The chances kept coming but none were converted. Extra time loomed ominously when a long ball from Simunovic saw Wallace challenge Griffiths with the striker coming off best and away with the ball. He had to time to look up and stab the ball with the outside of his left boot through the legs of Hill. The on-rushing Dembélé met it with a delightfully deft touch from his trailing foot, diverting the ball through the legs of first Kiernan and then Gilks. It was a treble nutmeg! And the goal that put Celtic into the final.

Griffiths and Dembélé celebrated by rushing into the Celtic fans located near the corner flag in the main stand – the exact spot where Hibs players had partied after their historic Cup Final goal against Rangers five months earlier. This was proving to be something of a Hampden hoodoo for The Deadybears.

In the seasons since the liquidation of Rangers, some Celtic fans had expressed relief at their continuing absence from Scottish football's top flight and the lack of poison in the atmosphere at games. Fans of the current incarnation of RFC, on the rare moments they could be heard, demonstrated again at this game how they liked to immerse themselves in sectarian songs and chants about child abuse. The Celtic support responded superbly with a love song which had become an anthem following the centenary celebrations of the 1916 Easter Rising. 'Grace' tells the tragic story of Grace Gifford and her love for one of the leaders of the Rising, Joseph Plunkett. The song bellowed around Hampden in a glorious spell during the second half and kept re-surfacing after moments of action on the pitch. The message was clear: your hatred will not prevail.

Brendan Rodgers was now in his first cup final in Scotland at the first time of asking. Aberdeen would be Celtic's opponents after a 2-0 win over Morton in the other semi-final.

Celtic were now just one game away from claiming the 100th trophy in the club's long, illustrious history.

The diminishing credibility of Warbiola was stretched even further post-match when he suggested that the gap between the sides was 'narrowing.' Celtic could – and should – have won the game in a canter. The fact that it was taking so long for the penny to drop among the deluded merely reflected their innate, misplaced sense of superiority. One of the Billy Boys asked online after the game *"Why has the level of stamina and fitness dropped this season when that was an admirable quality last season?"* The fact that they were no longer pitting their wits against part-time joiners, decorators and firefighters hadn't appeared to cross his mind.

It was going to be a long, long season for The Gullibillies.

26 OCTOBER: ROSS COUNTY 0 CELTIC 4　　　　　　Y

A midweek away trip to Dingwall is a slog for Celtic fans, with many having to take a half-day off work to ensure arrival in time for kick-off. In recent years the Highlands have proven to be difficult terrain for most teams, including Celtic. Tonight was even harder, coming off the back of a draining Sunday semi-final. Brendan Rodgers decided to mix things up with eight changes from the team that had beaten Rangers. One of those changes was Kieran Tierney who would be out for two months due to an ankle injury sustained in training.

A mazy run and fine finish from Patrick Roberts meant that Celtic got off to a great start only three minutes in at Victoria Park. That was not a prelude to an easy away win though. Craig Gordon's left leg kept Boyce at bay brilliantly and in the second half the Celtic keeper again saved well, on the line this time, from Dow. It was the post that then rescued Celtic from a Davies header before, with quarter of an hour to go, Craig Gordon came close to being red-carded for a challenge on Boyce well outside the penalty box. Predictably, the cries of 'Off!' came loudest from the press box. Gordon survived with a yellow card.

Brendan rang the changes to secure the win: Dembélé, Sinclair and Bitton all coming on in the second half. Armstrong snatched a second goal seven minutes from the end with Sinclair and Dembélé adding one each in injury time.

The score line looked emphatic but the Bhoys had to fight hard for these three points. The improved fitness of this team compared to previous seasons was there for all to see – late goals were now a regular feature as the opposition tired in the face of Celtic's consistent possession of the ball.

It would be the wee hours of the morning before the Celtic support arrived home but we were now seven points clear at the top of the SPFL and the sound of 'Championees!' was still ringing in their ears as they made their way back down the A9.

29 OCTOBER: ABERDEEN 0 CELTIC 1　　　　　🏆

Three days later and it was another long trip north, this time to Pittodrie for a top of the table clash. This was now, on paper, our hardest away game. We had lost both games there in Ronny Deila's last season. This match would prove a true barometer of the improvements that Brendan Rodgers had made to the squad now he was four months into the job.

Stuart Armstrong and Scott Brown provided the guile and graft in Celtic's midfield in what was a tough encounter. Celtic pressed hard throughout most of the game and created twice as many shooting opportunities as The Dandies.

The breakthrough moment came midway through the first half. A Shay Logan headed clearance was picked up on the bounce by Tom Rogic outside the box. He controlled the ball high with his right foot and, just as the ball was about to touch the ground, his left foot curled it high beyond Joe Lewis and into the net.

It was a majestic piece of skill. The Australian lapped up the cheers of the jubilant Celtic fans in the South Stand as he jogged towards them tapping the Celtic crest on his jersey.

Celtic put Lewis under sustained attack in search of a second but the big Englishman continually foiled Dembélé and Sinclair especially. As the 90th minute approached Aberdeen came more and more into the game. Substitutes Rooney and Maddison were causing problems and Shinnie came close to equalising.

An incredible six minutes of added time were somehow found from beneath the magic Masonic apron and it was Craig Gordon who saved the day in the dying seconds when he magnificently stopped a mis-directed Sviatchenko header from crossing the line.

A vital away win in trying circumstances had left Celtic nine points clear of the pack at the top of the league. It was another excellent clean sheet for Craig Gordon whose performance levels had improved tremendously since the arrive of rival de Vries.

Having such a strong lead so early in October meant it was time for a cover version of an old Paul Le Guen classic:

Warburton's going to get the sack
WE WON THE LEAGUE
before the clocks went back!

Spirit of The Jungle:

CELTIC'S NORTH CURVE

Over two decades have passed since the famed Jungle enclosure at Celtic Park was demolished to make way for the all-seater stadium that now dominates Glasgow's eastern cityscape.

For years, the terracing that ran along the pitch and Janefield Street housed Celtic's choirbhoys, the most vocal, vehement and verbally-abusive among the support. Celtic players were serenaded while opponents were vilified; anthems were sung and chants, often inspired by hymns or pop tunes, were adapted to inspire, mock or celebrate. The Jungle achieved legendary status amongst football aficionados throughout the UK and beyond.

An unfortunate side-effect of all-seater stadia has been the dilution of the raucous atmospheres which make football unique. Standing and singing are vital ingredients in generating an ambience that exists beyond just goal celebrations, which get everyone up on their feet. They are also at the core of 'ultra' fan culture which has spread from Italy and South America throughout the global game.

Celtic's main ultras group, the Green Brigade, was formed back in 2006 and established a base at the back of Section 111 in the lower tier junction where the North Stand meets the Lisbon Lions Stand. There they could stand (although not without resistance from stewards at times) and sing as well as host the novel displays and banners they quickly gained a strong reputation for. Their numbers gradually grew, and Section 111 became the focal point for singing, chanting and even dancing (choreography being a new phenomenon of fan culture!) at the modern Celtic Park.

The commitment of this section (dominated by the large ULTRAS CELTIC banner on the back wall) to standing and 'lateral movement' led to occasional conflict with the club but, through positive dialogue with the GB, officials were eventually persuaded that there was value in the creation of a safe standing area in the ground.

The next step was to persuade Glasgow City Council to approve the idea. As the local authority it is their responsibility to issue a safety certificate for the ground. In the aftermath of the Hillsborough Disaster, the passing of the Football Spectators Act 1989 meant that standing was effectively banned at stadia in the top two tiers of English football. Yet this legislation was never applied to Scotland and individual councils north of the border can decide whether to allow safe standing areas or not.

The consultation between club and council, which started in 2011, was focused on the first application of its kind in Scotland. GCC's Safety Advisory Group repeatedly refused to accept the safe standing proposal. It was believed that Police Scotland, who had publicly expressed their opposition to the Green Brigade and a desire to 'crush' the ultra group, were the main obstacle. It took almost five years until approval was finally granted to enable the club to make the necessary structural changes in time for the 2016-17 season.

Information leaflets for members of The North Curve

Rail seating is the most popular form of safe standing in European football and it was this model which Celtic adopted. There are barriers about 3ft tall along each row in front and behind of the seats. The seats are locked into an upright position on the back rail (but are unlocked for UEFA games, although few choose to adhere to this). The rails prevent anyone falling forward or backwards and the area is restricted to allocated ticket holders, one per seat, which prevents overcrowding. At Celtic Park, the safe standing area has been dubbed *The North Curve* and has standing room for 2,900 season ticket holders.

Standing and seating options at the end of season charity game

The Green Brigade occupy the bottom part of the North Curve and organise up to 900 fans based in that area. Supporters elsewhere in the standing section area have been invited to become members of The North Curve at £10 per season and have input into the displays and other activities. It is hoped that long-term The North Curve section will develop into a bloc of fans who also congregate together at away grounds too.

The friendly against Wolfsburg in July 2016 was the first outing for the new safe standing area. What was most noticeable was that the GB now occupied the front rather than rear of the area and had created a platform for two capos (who lead the songs/chants with megaphones) and drummers at either side.

This meant the noise flowed back upwards from the pitch and gave everyone in the section a clear point to focus on. As one visiting Liverpool fan later wrote: *"At the front of the section, two lads sacrifice much of their game-watching to cajole and choreograph, kicking off a songbook celebrating club, manager and players stretching through the duration of the match."*

This has been an inspired move. A concentration of those singing and chanting at the front has meant that songs now spread much quicker throughout the rest of section and out across the stadium. Last season was marked not only by the highest average attendances in a few years but by a much-improved atmosphere at home games with more seated fans throughout the ground (even the Main Stand) joining in.

The creation of the North Curve has also meant a larger space for the GB to use for their impressive displays. The Champions League Qualifier against Lincoln Red Imps saw the first display centred on the new section and it conveyed what the North Curve was aiming for: recreating the old spirit of The Jungle. It was the first in a series of outstanding displays throughout the season.

A flare for celebration: the North Curve salutes the Dembelition of Rangers

One of the most unusual and impressive displays in The North Curve's inaugural season was the idea to kit out the whole of the section with coloured ponchos for the visit of The Deadybears in September.

The huge banner above the section read 'They Hung Out The Flag of War' (from the famous rebel song The Foggy Dew) while below was a near 3000-strong human Irish tricolour. This magnificent sight was enhanced when it exploded into life on five different occasions as Brendan Rodgers' team destroyed the impoverished Ibrox outfit 5-1 thanks to an historic Moussa Dembélé hat-trick.

The Man City game at the end of September proved one of the most memorable. Taking the lead against the English champions on three separate occasions helped generate an incredible, frenzied atmosphere which the North Curve thrived on and kept on the boil throughout, with the rest of the stadium feeding off it. The noise that greeted Kieran Tierney's deflected goal reverberated well beyond Celtic Park through the city's east end.

The fierce tussle between the two teams saw six goals being shared and was complimented by the cacophony generated throughout, combining to make an unforgettable night of football. Celtic's new manager described it as *"a noise I've never heard before"* while his counterpart Pep Guardiola talked post-match of the thrill of playing Celtic de Glasgow and of Celtic Park being *"an amazing environment."*

Letting the moment linger: 'Grace' in the North Curve

The strongest testament to the success of the North Curve's first season has been the way that so many new songs have taken off with what was a fairly dormant home support in recent years. Celtic's away support has remained vibrant and vocal and it felt, at last, as though Celtic Park was stepping up to the mark again.

The Brendan Rodgers effect of course was a huge factor in what was to prove an outstanding debut campaign and the songs in honour of his key players – like Scott Sinclair, Stuart Armstrong and Moussa Dembélé – spread like wildfire around the stadium. The end-to-end chant of *Glasgow's Green & White* has never sounded better while anthems such as *'Grace'* and *The Fields of Athenry* are being sung with proper gusto around the whole stadium.

The club's brave decision to secure a standing area fuelled the atmosphere that helped drive the team to an incredible Treble. There was no doubt the team were lapping up the re-energised support from throughout the ground and especially in the North Curve.

Celtic beat off competition from England, South America and the USA to win the Fan Experience Award 2017 for the safe standing in practice and been impressed with the experience. One writer for *The Lad Bible* website said that where the singing was concerned *"the co-ordination is much-improved and the participation is far greater. That famed Celtic Park atmosphere doesn't happen by accident. Similarly, the standing environment seems to have galvanised the support into giving far more energy than in the past. There are almost no smart phones – the scourge of English Premier League grounds – with more people filming the singing than singing themselves. Indeed, the safe standing experience is almost completely safe and enjoyable."*

A memorable debut season for the North Curve was celebrated in style at the Hearts game in May when Celtic received the SPFL trophy for the 6th season in succession. The incredible stadium-wide Lisbon Lions tifo is mentioned in detail elsewhere in this book.

When it came to the 67th minute the Green Brigade led the chant of 'In the Heat of Lisbon' once again although this time, instead of the usual mobile phone light show, the North Curve revealed a number of lit flares in between huge green and white striped sheets covering the whole section.

The spectacular show was greeted with thunderous applause around the ground and proved a unique and glorious celebration of the Lions. The use of pyrotechnics within Celtic Park provoked the ire of the club and may not be repeated in the future yet it proved a memorable sign-off for what had been an unforgettable year in and out of the North Curve.

Here's to many more.

CHAPTER 5 — NOVEMBER
The fans came in their thousands

IN THE HEAT OF LISBON
THE FANS CAME IN THEIR THOUSANDS
TO SEE THE BHOYS BECOME
CHAMPIONS
SIXTY SEVEN

1 NOVEMBER: BORUSSIA MONCHENGLADBACH 1 CELTIC 1 🏆

It was back to Europe and an away tie against a certain German team just three days after the Pittodrie victory. Away games in Germany have long been savoured by the Celtic support and this was the first competitive fixture since a trip to Hamburg to play HSV in 2009. It was estimated that almost six thousand Tims headed across the North Sea, most of them based in nearby Dusseldorf, to enjoy the pre-match hospitality. Only 2,500 tickets were available in the Celtic section at the 46,000-capacity Borussia-Park stadium.

This was a much improved performance by Celtic from the home leg. Celtic looked better organised and played with more conviction. Scott Sinclair almost grabbed the lead when a beautiful curling shot from outside the box beat keeper Sommer but went glancing off the post to safety. Sommer saved well from Dembélé before Korb put BMG ahead just after the half-hour mark in a well-worked move which should have been better defended. Celtic didn't lose heart though, managing to retain majority possession in the game.

Monchengladbach keep the joke going in the away leg

In the 2nd half, Andre Hahn's first-time effort on 65 minutes was saved by the woodwork to deny the German side a two goal cushion. Ten minutes later, an inch-perfect pass from Roberts sent Dembélé through only for him to be pulled down in the box by goal-scorer Korb, who received a red card. The 20-year old Frenchman sent Sommer the wrong way to square the game with a quarter of an hour left and grab his 16th goal of the season (and third in the Champions League).

With little time on the clock, Roberts threaded a beautiful pass through to McGregor who was left one-on-one with the keeper – only for the midfielder to drag the ball past the far post. His anguished expression was reflected on the faces of the Celtic fans around the stadium.

Celtic had to make do with a point which meant they remained bottom of the group with only two points, yet confidence was taken from a decent performance. This was only the third time we'd avoided defeat in an away game in the Champions League group stages. It wasn't the much-vaunted day when we win away, but we were getting closer.

5 NOVEMBER: CELTIC 3 INVERNESS CALEY THISTLE 0 ♟

This game saw a visit to Celtic Park from the only Scottish team to have taken any points off Celtic in the league so far this season. ICT again proved difficult opponents. Despite playing both Dembélé and Griffiths, Celtic struggled to break the Highlanders down and Celtic's usual free-flowing style was impeded.

The teams went in 0-0 at half-time although it was only three minutes into the second half before a chipped McGregor pass was converted by Scott Sinclair for his 10th goal of the season. More and more cracks began to appear in the ICT defence and it was a driving run from McGregor (ended viciously by Tansey who was red-carded) that set up Dembélé whose shot was saved, only for Griffiths to bury the rebound. Sensibly, referee Allan had played on and Celtic reaped the benefits. Against 10 men there was now even more space for Celtic to exploit.

Tom Rogic sealed a 3-0 victory 7 minutes from the end, rounding off a great week for the team. 10 points clear – and It's Not New Year!

The week before this game, the former Rangers goalkeeper Peter McCloy revealed what we'd known for a long time was keeping fans of The Deady Bears awake at night. He told a newspaper that he *"fears Celtic winning 10 in a row."* It is good to know that we are dominating their nightmares as well as their waking hours. There was some off-field humiliation too for Scotland's Shame FC this week when their star striker Martyn Waghorn was filmed challenging a schoolboy to a fight after he'd received some cheeky comments. The funniest thing about the incident was that the professional footballer was having a take-away from a chip shop for his lunch. Such impressive dietary control helped explain his inability to transfer his lower-league form to the SPFL where he looked so far out of depth he should have been wearing scuba gear.

The day after the Inverness game saw Celtic fans gather at an important landmark in Glasgow's East End central to the club's story. St. Mary's Church in Abercromby Street in the Calton hosted a Mass on the 129th anniversary of the club's founding to celebrate Celtic's principal founder Brother Walfrid and the club's its association with the parish. It was after attending Mass on 6th November 1887 that a group retired to the old parish hall a few streets behind the church and took the decision to establish Celtic Football Club.

Father Tom White of St. Mary's and the Celtic FC Foundation organised the event where the Foundation's Christmas appeal was promoted with the aim of providing meals and gifts for 250 local families in poverty. The Mass was well attended by those of various faiths and none and was a great chance to reconnect with the parish where the club was founded as well as a timely reminder of the charitable reasons why Celtic came into being. It also provided an opportunity for supporters outside the parish to see the stunning mosaic celebrating the club's foundation which was kindly paid for by major shareholder Dermot Desmond following Celtic's 125th anniversary Mass at St Mary's.

It was Friday night football and time for a jaunt to Rugby Park after yet another international break. The resurgence in support for Celtic under Brendan was again demonstrated by the fact that both the opposing Moffat and Chadwick Stands were full of Tims. Celtic were in the pink – quite literally – with the awful third strip being worn. This monstrosity was supposedly Lisbon-inspired (spuriously based on the colour of the match ticket) but the very idea of John Clark or Tommy Gemmell wearing anything that colour on a football field was comical.

Dedryck Boyata was back in the Celtic side for the first time under the new manager and was looking to resurrect his career in the way that James Forrest and others had done. Forrest almost opened the scoring with a great curler of a shot which Jamie McDonald saved with some style. Killie were holding Celtic back but a break-through came just before half-time. Dembélé played the ball through to Armstrong, making a bursting run on the right side of the box, and he slammed it home to give Celtic the lead. He was back in great form and proving to the new manager how important a part he could play in his team. And he didn't have a hair out of place.

The second half was a towsy affair and Celtic struggled to add to the lead. Brendan Rodgers had already made clear his dislike of artificial surfaces. His opinion wasn't changed by this experience. Kilmarnock came close a couple of times and Boyata had to make a goal-line clearance to keep the clean sheet. A Lustig effort came off the post late on but Celtic had to make do with the solitary goal. It was another determined performance and three points won where they might have been squandered in previous seasons.

With the festive season just around the corner it was only right and proper that the fans at Rugby Park resurrected the old favourite 'Last Christmas' with Brendan now replacing Ronny in our affections. Inside the ground I heard a boy behind me tell his pal that he'd driven past a Rangers pub at Bridgeton Cross at the weekend and all the smokers outside were sporting moustaches for the 'Movember' charity. *"Fair play to the Huns"* the guy said *"but I hope their husbands try it next year as well."*

The festive spirit was alive and well back at Celtic Park where the club launched its Christmas shopping campaign with a bizarre video featuring Broony in a onesie and a shrunken Leigh Griffiths in an elf's outfit with giant ears sitting on a mantlepiece. It was like a special Celtic episode of The Magic Roundabout.

23 NOVEMBER: CELTIC 0 BARCELONA 2

Celtic Park was full for the return of frequent visitors Barcelona in the 5th group match in the Champions League. After the annihilation in the Nou Camp, Celtic were looking to regain some respect and this was achieved with a much more combative performance. The tone was set early on when Scott Brown dumped Sergio Busquets on his arse, much to the approval of the home support (later in the game, a swivel of Messi's hips was enough to put Broony on his own arse as he attempted to tackle the little Argentinian; my two kids were genuinely amazed at the skill on show).

Matching the Catalan giants over 90 minutes would prove a more difficult task though. It was just after the half-way point in the first half when a delightful bending chip from Neymar was converted by Messi, with four Celtic players at hand but all bewildered by the pace of the move. Soon after Craig Gordon made a superb one-handed save from a Suarez header to keep Celtic in the game. An enforced change saw Sinclair replaced by Forrest at half-time.

It was an excellent Forrest cross, taking out four defenders to set up Dembélé, which created Celtic's best chance of the night – only for it to be spurned as it was met with a tame header. It was all over for Celtic when Messi scored from the penalty spot in the 55th minute, ending any flickering hopes of qualification. The Argentinian had scored five goals against the Hoops in just two games – one more than the entire Rangers team would manage in six games against us this season.

One significant talking point of the night was the behaviour of Neymar who got a yellow card for a foul on Lustig and was lucky not to get a red in a further incident with Celtic's Swede.

Coach Luis Enrique hooked the Brazilian before his petulance resulted in dismissal. Barca would eventually get knocked out at the quarter final stage by Juventus in what was ultimately a disappointing season for the Catalan team. After this game an angry Celtic fan tweeted Neymar Junior to express his disgust at his behaviour and ended the diatribe with some Glaswegian goodwill: *"I hope yer next shite is a hedgehog."*

Throughout this 50th anniversary season of the triumph of the Lions in Lisbon, home and away, evening games were illuminated in the 67th minute when thousands of mobile phone lights were switched on as the fans chanted In the Heat of Lisbon. Tonight, for my money, was the best of these light shows with every stand in Paradise aglow with thousands upon thousands of sparkling lights. A remarkable tribute to a remarkable group of players.

Celtic Park lit up in honour of the Lions

27 NOVEMBER: ABERDEEN 0 CELTIC 3

The first cup final in Brendan Rodgers' reign as Celtic manager was to prove a memorable occasion. Aberdeen were quietly confident that they would cause an upset having emerged as Celtic's main challengers in the League. Winning the League Cup had added significance for Celtic as the immense green, white and gold display that stretched across the entire Celtic End at Hampden before kick-off demonstrated: the 100th trophy in the club's history was the target.

A Dembélé header quickly tested Joe Lewis in the Aberdeen goal but it was a surging run from Jozo Simunovic in 15 minutes that led to Celtic's opener. Despite almost losing the ball he managed to find Rogic on the right side of the box and the Australian swept the ball from there all the way past Lewis into the bottom corner for a glorious opener. Although he rarely finished a game, the Aussie continually produced moments of genius like this to merit his inclusion in the starting 11.

It was just over 20 minutes later when a Rogic pass found James Forrest in the centre circle. The Ayrshire bhoy surged forward and the Aberdeen defence backed off him until he broke into the box, did a delightful shimmy and then smacked a right foot shot past Lewis to make it 2-0. As we celebrated around Hampden it felt as though there was no way back for the Sheepies.

It was James Forrest, in an impressive all-round display, who struck the final nail in Aberdeen's coffin early in the second half. Another surging run of his ended when he was scythed down by O'Connor in the box. Moussa Dembélé stepped up to slot away another penalty – it was 3 and easy now for Celtic.

The free style with which Celtic were playing was a joy to behold. Hampden appearances had become a lottery for us in recent years but the professionalism shown today under the new manager suggested a corner had been turned. Aberdeen were left chasing our tails throughout. Significantly, it was another clean sheet - which meant over two months had passed since Celtic had lost a single goal domestically.

The League Cup had also become a bit of a bogey trophy for us in recent years – 30 final appearances had yielded only 15 wins before today. This 16th success, allied to 47 League titles, 36 Scottish Cups and 1 European Cup meant it was 100 up for the Celts.

A great video emerged later that day on social media of Bertie Auld, standing on a table in an executive box in the Main Stand at Hampden, pressed up against the glass, celebrating with the Celtic fans in front of him, mimicking the knock-out blow his team had just delivered to the Dons. This was a man who'd personally contributed to a fair number of the 100 trophies we'd won – and he was loving it as much as we were!

That evening, at the front door of Celtic Park, as Brendan stood before a large illuminated 'CFC 100' sign, there was genuine emotion in his voice as he told the assembled supporters: *"As a manager of a club that I've supported all my life ... to win that first trophy means a lot to us but it obviously means everything to you as well."* Incredibly, this was the first major piece of silverware that Brendan had ever won in the game. At his press conference there was no doubting the significance of the moment to him: *"I am proud to be the manager of Celtic and to bring a trophy to the people I love, the club I support and the players."*

CHAPTER 6 – DECEMBER
To save me from tears

LAST CHRISTMAS
I GAVE YOU MY HEART
BUT THE VERY NEXT DAY
YOU GAVE IT AWAY

THIS YEAR
TO SAVE ME FROM TEARS
I'LL GIVE IT TO
BRENDAN RODGERS

Nine games were crammed into the month of December and it was the first of those, a lunchtime fixture away at Fir Park, which was to prove one of the season's most memorable – and provide a feast of goals for those Celtic fans in the South and Main Stands. The day started off in sadness though with a minute's silence to commemorate those who had died in the recent Chapecoense plane disaster in Brazil.

There was little to fear at Fir Park, or so it seemed, given that Motherwell had lost 3-0 at Tynecastle the previous weekend and Celtic's defence had been in imperious form. Going in 2-0 down at half-time came as a huge shock for Celtic players and fans alike – as did the goals themselves. It was only three minutes in when Louis Moult superbly lobbed Craig Gordon after a floated pass from ex-Celt Stephen McManus. Then, just after the half-hour, Moult converted a cross at the back post with no little skill to put Celtic in real trouble. For the first time in a long time, Celtic looked uneasy and a first domestic defeat of the season was on the cards.

Brendan made a tactical switch for the second half, going with three at the back. Callum McGregor had already replaced Izaguirre and was now moved forward to midfield. This brought an immediate dividend when he played a neat one-two with Armstrong and sallied into the heart of the Motherwell defence, sent a defender the wrong way and slotted the ball past Samson. The comeback was on. Twelve minutes later Stuart Armstrong glided in from the left flank and floated across a perfect ball to the back past where Paddy Roberts was charging in unmarked to head home the equaliser. Now the momentum was with Celtic.

Or so we thought. Just a minute later Motherwell were back on the attack and Hammill mirrored what Armstrong had just done and this time Ainsworth, unmarked at the back post, converted with ease to put them 3-2 ahead. This was a real sickener. Celtic had done everything to get back in the game and now we had it all to do again.

From the resultant kick-off, Paddy Roberts burst forward with the ball. He saw a darting run from Armstrong behind Henaghen and picked him out perfectly. The midfielder collected the ball with his right foot and hit it on the turn beyond Samson and into the net. 3-3! Three goals in just three minutes. What a game this was.

There was just over a quarter of an hour left and Celtic continued to probe and press for a winner, but to no avail. Time was running out and Motherwell were clearly tiring yet, in all honesty, it felt as though a point had been rescued and defeat averted which was the main thing.

And then, in the dying seconds of injury time, Forrest fed the ball from the left wing in to Rogic. He took a couple of touches forward, moving the ball to the edge of the box, then – as two challenges were coming in - he swung his right foot and drilled the ball into the opposite corner of the net! He had won it – with seconds to spare! Four goals to three.

Here We Go - 10 in a Row! Celtic fans celebrate the amazing comeback at Fir Park

Why settle for one point when you can have all three?!? All around the fans were going absolutely tonto. This was how to win a game. Some supporters joined the players pitch-side as the celebrations spilled over from the stand. What a scene of jubilation it was.

The final whistle had blown. The South Stand was rocking to the chant of *'Here we go – 10 in a row!'* as the joyous players made their way towards it to take the acclaim of the fans. Everyone seemed to be holding ten fingers in the air and bouncing with joy. Winning this game, after being behind 3 times, meant we could win any game. We were beginning to feel unbeatable.

The singing continued. Brendan Rodgers was serenaded with a chorus of 'Last Christmas' as he waved at the fans. One of his most valued players was missing from the scenes of celebration on the pitch – but that was because Kieran Tierney was up in the top tier, cheering on his team-mates.

When news of his presence spread, fans started chanting his name as well.

An incredible Celtic comeback had harvested four top-drawer goals. One of the best things about them was that Keith Lasley, Motherwell's hammer thrower par excellence, had supreme close-up views of each one. The pain etched on his face at the final whistle was delicious to see! We had overcome numerous set-backs to emerge victorious in a glorious seven-goal thriller. Who could stop us on this form?

6 DECEMBER: MANCHESTER CITY 1 CELTIC 1

Over 4,000 Celtic supporters made the trip to Manchester for the final tie in this year's Champions League competition, even though qualification was no longer possible. With the official allocation being less than 3,000 inevitably some Celtic fans ended up in the home end of the Emptihad where they sung regardless. The previous game against Pep Guardiola's team had been one of the most exciting in years and Celtic were confident of putting on another good show.

The game was only 4 minutes old when Patrick Roberts demonstrated to his employers exactly why Celtic fans had been raving about him. Cutting in from the right, he showed tremendous footwork to get round a Man City colleague and then fire the ball home to give Celtic an early lead. City, who had made nine changes from their game at the weekend, were quick to respond and Iheanacho outstripped Simunovic and beat Gordon with a fierce shot. Dembélé missed a decent chance soon after an excellent, mazy run from Forrest.

Griffiths and (the rarely seen) Mackay-Steven spurned opportunities to score in the second-half. The Celtic fans made themselves heard throughout the Etihad in what proved a decent game for what was effectively a dead rubber.

Celtic held their own against an albeit weakened City side, finishing the group in bottom slot with 3 points from 6 games. There had been some harsh lessons along the way but also signs of development. Focus now turned exclusively to domestic matters.

9 DECEMBER: PARTICK THISTLE 1 CELTIC 4   ♟

A freezing cold Firhill on a Friday night wouldn't normally get the romantic juices flowing. Yet, for two fellow Tims in the queue for the Jackie Husband Stand, it was enough to get them singing all the verses of Wham's festive anthem Last Christmas in adoration of Brendan Rodgers.

Glasgow's answer to George Michael and Andrew Ridgeley helped pass the time as the familiar Firhill delays were in evidence which meant kick off was about to be missed for many in the queue. That was until one enterprising Tim persuaded a steward to open an exit gate for a brief moment – allowing a few hundred fans the chance to flood through with tickets intact.

On the park, Leigh Griffiths was back leading the line for only the third time this season. An injury in August and the arrival of Dembélé – and his goals – had restricted the appearances of Celtic's No.9 but he showed what we'd been missing tonight.

Alan Archibald's Thistle team had progressed in the League and were no pushovers. It took until five minutes before the interval for Celtic to break down Thistle's resistance. Griffiths' fought hard to deliver a ball right across the face of goal which Armstrong stabbed home. Early in the second half it was two for Stu when he venomously struck a ball from over 25 yards out which skipped past Cerny on the way into the net. More and more he was showing what a quality player he was.

From the resulting kick-off, Celtic immediately pressed and Gamboa won back possession. He then started a move which saw the ball filtered through to Griffiths who spun defender Barton superbly, putting him on his jacksie, and then beat Cerny with a precise shot. The wee man looked as delighted with his goal as the fans were.

Thistle pulled one back from an unmarked header and almost repeated the trick five minutes later but it was chalked off by the referee for offside. It was a scare but 15 minutes later Celtic closed off the game. Great work from Izaguerre set up McGregor to slot home Celtic's 4th and extend the gap to 11 points over Rangers in second place.

It had been a boisterous Celtic support throughout with many seemingly still on the sauce from Manchester. They celebrated not only the prospect of winning this League title but the idea of going on to make it '10'. Here we go, indeed.

'I'll give it to Brendan Rodgers'

13 DECEMBER: CELTIC 1 HAMILTON 0   Y

The unfamiliar light blue of the Accies' away jersey was met with the equally uncommon sight of Celtic playing with two strikers, a rare combination under Brendan Rodgers' charge. Dembélé and Griffiths tried hard and linked up well without ever looking like a proper partnership. Griffiths owed thanks to the Frenchman when he unselfishly passed to him after a great through ball from Rogic. The chance was almost lost but Griffiths managed to convert and give Celtic the lead 35 mins in.

It was one of the highlights on a cold and quiet night at Celtic Park. Hamilton fought well and contained Celtic for long periods. Former Celt Mo Mo Massimo Donati had a decent chance from a corner in the first half while Eamon Brophy almost grabbed a late equaliser for the Accies four minutes from time following a defensive mix up, his shot just going wide of the post.

It was a scrappy and uncomfortable performance at times and it likely left the manager unpersuaded of the value in playing two up front very often after this experience.

17 DECEMBER: CELTIC 2 DUNDEE 1   Y

Dundee were next up Paradise in an usual trio of home games. Paul Hartley's team, still struggling near the relegation zone, were happy to concede possession and play on the counter-attack in the hope of snatching a point. It was a plan that almost worked.

Leigh Griffiths was the man preferred up front for Celtic. One early effort from him hit a post but it took until injury time in the first half before the Dundee defence was breached. A poor Darren O'Dea challenge on Rogic (which led to a yellow card and the Socceroo having to be replaced) allowed Griffiths the opportunity to swerve the dead ball over the wall and out of the reach of keeper Bain – the balding front man again showing terrific technique. Nir Bitton doubled Celtic's tally on the 57th minute when he passed the ball into the net from 20 yards out in a strike stunning in its simplicity.

Goals and appearances were rare for the Israeli but he served up a peach here.

Dundee pulled one back 10 minutes later through Haber before El Bakhtaoui, a late substitute, sauntered through the Celtic defence and chipped a shot over the bar when it looked easier to hit the net. It was another lucky late break for Celtic but it meant we had now gone 20 games unbeaten in Scotland.

20 DECEMBER: CELTIC 1 PARTICK THISTLE 0   ♻

A soaking wet Tuesday night in December and it was Partick Thistle again, only nine days on from the last encounter against the Jags and Celtic's 4th game in 10 days. On nights like this it is all about getting a result.

Although sitting bottom of the league, Thistle were only two points off eighth-placed Motherwell. They were on a poor run of results but again caused Celtic problems and proved difficult to overcome. Brendan Rodgers made eight changes to Celtic's line up, bringing in Liam Henderson for a rare appearance and also giving a debut to 18-year-old Calvin Miller at left-back. He acquitted himself well and showed a good touch coming forward.

Scott Sinclair broke the deadlock 16 minutes in when he finished superbly after great work from Henderson. Other chances came and went, with Dembélé most prominent, and Thistle also could have scored. It ended up another single goal victory, the 3rd in succession, but importantly it meant we were now 16 points clear. Not pretty, but very effective.

Something else which wasn't pretty was an unruly ruck between online PsychoBillies and fans of the teen girl group Little Mix. Deidco's delirious followers had decided to try and get the song Glad All Over by The Dave Clark Five to the Christmas No.1 spot. This was because in recent months they'd altered the words of that song into a truly awful chant in which they made the spurious claim that We've got (clap clap) Joey Garner in honour of their overweight and under-achieving centre-forward.

Little Mix had a song of their own out which their fans were pushing to be the festive No.1 and the dignified hordes ended up in a rammy with teenage girls all over social media as to which song was the best.

Unsurprisingly, the girl group made it No.4 in the Xmas chart while the Sevconians admirably forced their song all the way up the Top 40 to ... number 31. It had ultimately proved as successful as their Going for 55 campaign slogan which has slowly but surely disappeared from sight as this season had progressed. It would turn out to be a painful festive season for the hefty English striker in other ways...

24 DECEMBER: HAMILTON 0 CELTIC 3　　　　　　　Y

It was Christmas Eve and those Celtic fans who had evaded the drunk tank enjoyed a festive time at a misty and dark New Douglas Park. Kieran Tierney was the main attraction on the way into the ground, having photos taken and giving autographs to his fellow fans. Although he had been missed, his team-mates continued to grind out wins but today showed a return to form and the style of football the manager was looking to embed.

Sviatchenko almost got the festive celebrations underway 4 minutes in but his header was cleared off the line. Both teams had chances but it was Leigh Griffiths who made the difference. A great pass from McGregor just before the break set the striker free and he coolly slotted the ball past Woods before indulging the fans with a Henrik Larsson-style celebration. It was the last we would see of him though as he was subbed at half time for Dembélé due to a calf injury.

Willie Collum cast himself in the role of *The Grinch Who Tried To Steal Celtic's Christmas* when he sent off Callum McGregor for a second innocuous offence just after the start of the second half. It was the kind of inexplicable decision that this referee has made a career out of. Ten-man Celtic responded to the setback in some style seven minutes later when Stuart Armstrong fired in a sensational strike from 25 yards to give Celtic a commanding lead.

It was his seventh goal of the season and yet another gem.

Celtic controlled the rest of the game and, with five minutes remaining, Forrest combined neatly with Dembélé to make it 3-0. Celtic's unbeaten run continued, despite Willie Collum's best efforts.

New Douglas Park on the eve of the apocalypse, apparently

28 DECEMBER: CELTIC 2 ROSS COUNTY 0 ♟

The relentless grind of games in December continued with a visit from Ross County. The Victoria Park team were again enjoying a decent season, sitting sixth in the league. Leigh Griffiths again led the Celtic line and Ryan Christie was back in the team in what was to prove an eye-catching performance.

County defended in numbers, as expected, and it took a while for Celtic to wear them down. It was the 38th minute before Scott Fox was beaten and it came from an unlikely source. Erik Sviatchenko donned the mantle of Beckenbauer as he strode out of defence and unleashed a right foot shot from 40 yards which bobbled in just the right places on its way past Fox. A second goal followed soon after when Armstrong turned a defender one way, then the other, then another by which point the ball was already on its way to the far corner of the net. As the song says, he scores belters all the time.

Celtic had done what was needed. The second half offered little more in the way of excitement and there were no more goals. It was another professional performance and minds were already turning to Saturday's top of the league clash against Warbiola's Warriors, who had helpfully just dropped points away in a draw at McDiarmid Park.

Celtic had now gone unbeaten at Celtic Park in domestic games throughout the whole of 2016. The ground was turning into a fortress again. All the omens were pointing towards a happy Hogmanay for those in the Hoops.

31 DECEMBER: RANGERS 1 CELTIC 2 ♢

This was Celtic's first visit to Ibrox in over four years following the liquidation of the old club. After years of financial neglect, their stadium was looking more tarnished than their support's reputation. Mark Warburton's team had not lost at home since September 2015 (as the media constantly reminded us) and were Celtic's closest challengers, although already trailing by 15 points. We also had a game in hand.

Dark clouds over the Debtdome: Celtic fans visit Ibrokes for the first time since March 2012

Celtic started the game poorly and looked weak down the flanks. In the 12th minute, Izaguirre was beaten comfortably for pace by Tavernier whose cross was slotted home by the ageless and still hopeless Kenny Miller.

Celtic responded well and Armstrong's looping pass sent Sinclair through and, after an initial stumble, he fired off a shot which came off the inside of Foderingham's far post before Hill scrambled the ball clear.

The resulting corner kick landed at the feet of Dembélé and he absolutely smashed the ball into the roof the net with a left-foot howitzer to equalise. The shot was struck with the kind of venom Rangers fans reserve for the Gallant Pioneer Craig Whyte and Dembélé had scored his fifth goal against the Ibrox club in just three games. The Broomloan Stand shook in celebration as 7000 Tims went ballistic. Not a few Celtic fans had wondered whether the down-at-heel stadium, which was considered in certain quarters to be unsafe, would withstand their joyous exertions.

Celtic looked more composed after the break as the team attacked in the direction of the Broomloan. Our dominance slowly grew. A McGregor cross was met by a downward volley from Dembélé which beat Foderingham but came back off the crossbar, with Sinclair missing the follow-up. It was a different story in the 70th minute when Roberts danced past McKay on the right wing and set up Armstrong. His pass across the face of goal was turned in by Sinclair, sparking fresh scenes of jubilation in the Free Broomloan. Kenny Miller spurned a last-minute chance to equalise when he hit the same post that Sinclair had in the first half.

Before this game the Rangers striker Joe Garner (he of Top 31 fame) had boasted that he would bully Celtic's defenders. There was much hilarity then when he had to be subbed only 15 minutes in after coming off worse in an aerial challenge with Sviatchenko. The hilarity grew later that night when a photo emerged of him sitting in the waiting room of the A&E at the Southern General hospital in full Rangers kit and wearing a pair of flip-flops awaiting treatment for his sore shoulder. New words for the Joey Garner song were quickly found...

Celtic had re-asserted their dominance over Warbiola's team and were now an impressive 19 points clear before New Year with a game still in hand. The party in the Broomloan was in full swing as Scott Brown carried the injured Leigh Griffiths on his back towards the fans, Celtic scarf twirling, to join the celebrations in the goalmouth. The forward then tied the scarf to the Ibrox post to demonstrate that Glasgow truly belonged to us.

CHAPTER 7 – JANUARY
Build a bonfire

BUILD A BONFIRE
BUILD A BONFIRE
PUT THE RANGERS ON THE TOP
PUT THE JAM TARTS IN THE MIDDLE
AND WE'LL BURN THE F**KING LOT!

The Ibrox victory on Hogmanay was the last Celtic action we'd see for some weeks as the winter break had returned to Scottish football. This meant there would be only 3 games in January as Brendan and the Celtic squad enjoyed a relaxing break and some light training on the beaches of Dubai.

Business was still going on back at Celtic Park and Ivory Coast international midfielder Eboue Kouassi signed for £3m from the Russian club Krasnodar. Although aged only 19 he already had experience of European competition and was considered an excellent prospect for the future. The Irish defender Eoghan O'Connell left the club after being sold to Walsall and Ryan Christie was surprisingly loaned out to our main domestic challengers, Aberdeen.

'Fake news' was to become a hot topic in 2017 however it was one of the few things that the Scottish sports press were already expert at. One fine example was the story from Keith Jackson (laughingly the Scottish Sports News Writer of the Year) that 'Rangers starlet' Barrie McKay was a £6million signing target for RB Leipzig following a friendly between the clubs.

This is the kind of stuff that the Bares lap up and it of course helps to push up the value of the player by generating interest, much to the benefit of the selling club. Or so you would think. The fact that McKay later joined Nottingham Forest for less than £500,000 confirms that such dubious strategies don't always work.

There was more fake news after the transfer window closed when Warbiola warbled that *"I could have signed 15 players this January but wanted quality over quantity."* It says much about the state of Scottish football writing that they merely re-hash such nonsense without question. Warbiola's outpourings were increasingly on a par with the North Korean leader Kim Jong-un yet slavishly reported all the same.

Thank God the actual football was back...

22 JANUARY: ALBION ROVERS 0 CELTIC 3

Celtic's Scottish Cup campaign got underway with a visit to Airdrie. Kieran Tierney was back in a Celtic jersey against Coatbridge's finest (the game was played at Airdrie's Excelsior Stadium to accommodate a bigger crowd) and he set up Sinclair for an exquisite lob to give the Bhoys a 30-minute lead. Albion had a packed defence and midfield designed to soak up the inevitable Celtic pressure. Brendan Rodgers again fielded a strong Celtic side rather than tempt fate and the continual proddings of Armstrong and Roberts undid Albion's hard work. A great Roberts run led to a Brown cross which was converted by a Dembélé knee in the 77th minute. Armstrong was the at the end of another mazy Roberts run to make it 3-0 at the game's death.

Mission accomplished.

25 JANUARY: CELTIC 1 ST JOHNSTONE 0

Celtic's return to League duty was this midweek game in hand against St Johnstone which also marked Scott Brown's 400th appearance for the club. It proved a typically robust and inspiring performance from the Celtic captain as the Perth club put up a strong show of resistance.

The key figure in the game was Dedryck Boyata, making only his third appearance of the season. He almost put the Celts in the lead before Wotherspoon cleared his effort off the line. He then earned warm applause after haring all the way back to his own penalty box and producing an expertly-timed slide tackle to deny Kane. This appeared to be a confident and competent Boyata, much removed from his first season in the Hoops.

St Johnstone made it to the second-half all square but Celtic began to impose themselves and create more chances. A brave Boyata header from a well-delivered Armstrong corner finally gave Celtic the lead in the 72nd minute – and the three points were ours. That meant a 22 point gap at the top – or chasm, to be more exact.

It was a memorable night for the Celtic captain but it was almost ruined by a teuchter sitting behind me who kept referring to him as 'Brownie' like something you would buy from Greggs along with a yum yum. The perpetual greeting face of Steven McLean being on the end of yet another defeat by Celtic helped make up for it though.

At the end of January in Scotland there are often Burns Nights organised in the memory of the world-renowned poet, Rabbie Burns. Friday 27th January 2017 saw Celtic Park celebrate a flame-haired genius whose poetry was mostly contained in his left-foot as The Tommy Burns Supper was held in Paradise for the first time.

This was an event started by the Heriot-Watt CSC in Edinburgh in the 1980s and was revived here in order to benefit the skin cancer charity that Tommy's family set up following his tragic death in 2008. The Kerrydale Suite played host to a fantastic night celebrating this unique Celtic son. Friends and team-mates who took to the stage to share memories of Tommy included Packie Bonner, Peter Grant, Gordon Strachan, Billy Stark, Tom Boyd and Tosh McKinlay.

There was a surprise appearance from Brendan Rodgers who was roundly cheered to the rafters as he talked of his friendship with Tommy from their time at Reading. The political journalist Bernard Ponsonby also shared stories of Tommy and his time as a Celtic supporter. It was Gordon Strachan who stole the show with some choice language and very funny stories.

The best of which was his well-timed revenge on a bluenose garage attendant working on London Road in the 2008 title run-in.

The night finished with a video of Tommy singing his favourite song 'Mack the Knife' which had everyone on their feet. A fantastic total of £15,000 was raised from this joyful night in memory of the Bhoy from the Calton.

29 JANUARY: CELTIC 4 HEARTS 0 ♛

A warm welcome awaited Hearts and their new manager Ian Cathro. He had been appointed despite having no management experience and looked like someone who had just been promoted to manager in a McDonald's restaurant. His ill-judged post-match interviews were already the stuff of legend. It was a warm welcome in the sense that everyone was urged to build a bonfire, put the Jam Tarts in the middle after putting the Rangers on the top and then burn the f**king lot. Welcome to Paradise Ian!

Today was an opportunity for Brendan Rodgers' men to make history: victory would mean that they had beaten the Lisbon Lions' record of 26 unbeaten domestic matches which had stood for 50 years. In contrast, Cathro's team had only won 2 out of the 7 games since he took over from Robbie Neilson and expectations were low – even though Celtic were missing Dembélé, Griffiths and Armstrong through injury.

An excellent Callum McGregor run and finish gave Celtic a 29th minute lead. Kieran Tierney was back to his best down Celtic's left side. He and Scott Sinclair had developed a formidable partnership over the course of the season. In the 77th minute a Tierney cross caused panic in the Hearts defence and Sinclair pushed it over the line. Three minutes on and Tierney tee'd up his pal Patrick Roberts for a smart left-foot finish. Celtic were home and dry. In injury time the youth Jack Aitchison was upended in the Hearts box and Sinclair smashed the resulting penalty past Hamilton. He couldn't seem to stop scoring against the Jambos.

An impressive 4-0 win without any recognised strikers and another record smashed by a resurgent Celtic team.

This season was getting better and better.

KT63

❋

I ONLY DREAMT ABOUT CELTIC

❋

It was a Hampden Roar like no other. With his right hand grasping the badge of his Celtic jersey and his left hand clutching the Scottish Cup, Kieran Tierney screamed in delight towards the Celtic support. He was not to be denied his moment of glory, or sharing it with the people he loved. Even a broken jaw couldn't stop him.

It was his fourth senior medal. He was now an internationalist. He had just won the SPFA and SFWA Young Player of the Year Awards for the 2nd year running. He stood as a key member of the record-breaking Invincibles team that had just won the Treble for the fourth time in Celtic's history. **And he was only 19 years old.**

There are few things that all Celtic fans agree on all of the time. Kieran Tierney is one of them. The absolute popularity of the left-back among the Celtic support is reminiscent of another era – as is the bhoy himself. The fact that he is unquestionably one of our own makes his success all the sweeter.

A young KT receiving Shunsuke Nakamura's boots after impressing in a training session

He has been attending Celtic games since the age of three with his father Michael. Hailing from Muirhouse in Motherwell, he never had eyes for another team: *"When you are younger some people dream about playing in the English Premier League. I only dreamt about Celtic. It was always a Celtic strip I wore."*

He has been a long-time member of his local Celtic Supporters Club and still attends games with them when he is injured, such as the 2016 League Cup semi-final against Rangers. In one of many interviews he gave in this season he said: *"My supporters' bus is the Wishaw Emerald CSC. Will they rename it after me? I don't deserve that yet, it's a classy bus."*

Kieran's Celtic credentials are impeccable. He attended Our Lady's High School in Motherwell where his mother Gail works and whose former pupils include Billy McNeill, Jimmy Johnstone, Bobby Murdoch and John Clark. He was scouted for Celtic by John McStay, the father of Paul, Willie and Raymond, when aged just seven whilst playing for his local team, Netherton Boys Club. He has been signed to Celtic ever since. When John McStay died in 2017, KT took to Twitter to express his sympathy and gratitude. Raymond McStay responded: *"Only one Celtic jersey made it on his wall and it wasn't any of ours! Thanks for your lovely tribute."*

KT in his early years at Celtic's academy

He was a ball boy at Celtic Park and had the best view in the stadium when Victor Wanyama scored against Barcelona in November 2012. Two years earlier he made an unusual appearance on camera in the aftermath of the Scottish Cup semi-final defeat to Ross County as his father vented the frustration we all felt at a truly dire Celtic performance. *"This is the future in front of us"* he said, pointing to Kieran and his young pals. How prophetic those words proved.

Yet the path to glory for KT has not always run smooth. He joined Celtic's academy – based at St Ninian's School in Kirkintilloch and the club's training facility at Lennoxtown – at the age of 13. This meant a change of school and a new regime: *"I was getting up at 6am, doing training then all your school work and then having to train again at night."*

Three years later and it wasn't certain that he would be kept on at the academy when it came to the crunch. *"There was a few years where I wasn't getting game time and I didn't know whether I would be offered a contract at that time, so it's hard. I don't think anybody really has a plain-sailing youth career but I dug deep and worked hard when I needed to."*

This tenacity would prove to be a recurring feature of Celtic's established left-back.

When Ronny Deila took charge of Celtic in the summer of 2014, left-footed Tierney caught his eye quickly. Having just turned 17, he featured in friendlies against Spurs and Villareal before being named on the first-team bench for a Ross County game on 27th December 2014.

He was due to head to Gran Canaria with the first team but a broken leg in a freak training ground accident meant he spent the New Year in Muirhouse wearing a moon boot. This would be a major setback for most, but the young Celt learnt from the experience: *"I've always said it was probably a good time to break my leg."*

"My confidence was high and I'd had a taste of it. It was a reality check. I just tried to work as hard as I could in the gym. I was only out for 6 to 8 weeks, which wasn't long for a leg break, so it all worked out well."

He didn't have to wait long for his first-team chance, replacing Emilio Izaguirre late on in a 2-1 win over Dundee at Dens Park on 22nd April 2015. Manager Deila was in no doubt about the value of tee-totaller Tierney: *"I wouldn't change Kieran Tierney for anyone. You see his attitude, it's always first class."* The reward for breaking into the first-team was a four-year professional contract.

Emilio was a popular player with the support and there was no real suggestion he would be permanently replaced as season 2015-16 got underway. KT continued to impress the management team in training and, when the Honduran faced suspension in the Europa League tie against Fenerbahce in October 2015, it was the young Scot rather than Man United loanee Tyler Blackett that they turned to. He impressed against the Turks, retained his place in the team, and his unforgiving tackling, strong running and excellent crossing were redeeming features in what was ultimately a disappointing season for Celtic.

He won his first international cap for Scotland against Denmark in March 2016 and ended the season with a League winner's medal and both Young Player of the Year Awards from his fellow professionals and the football scribes.

Celtic Park roared with delight on 15th May 2016 when it witnessed KT's first goal in the Hoops as he opened the scoring in a 7-0 victory over Motherwell. He cut in from his favoured position on the left and rifled the ball into the bottom corner of the net before a tackle could be made. He kissed the Celtic badge as he looked towards his family sitting in the Main Stand – another great moment for the scrap book.

In many respects he'd made it: he'd fulfilled most of our dreams and was still a teenager. He could have been forgiven for having a well-earned rest until pre-season training got underway with the new manager.

Instead, he hired a personal trainer and worked on improving his stamina levels while his team-mates sunned themselves abroad. This was the work ethic his parents had imbued in him. It bore immediate fruit when Brendan Rodgers ran his eye over the him for the first time: *"I saw in the first two days I was in charge that Kieran will be a top player. He has the right attitude and he's quicker than I thought. I had only seen him in highlights and clips before coming here, but when you see him close up, he's a super athlete. He's strong, quick, balanced and aggressive. He has a wonderful left foot and will get better."*

And of course, he has - as he demonstrated on the biggest stage of all.

It had been three long years, but Champions League nights returned to Celtic Park after KT and his team-mates survived a tumultuous away fixture against Hapoel Be'er Sheva. Losing seven goals in the Nou Camp won't be forgotten any time soon – *"a brutal experience and you never want to go through that in your career, so you learn from it"* – but it helped prepare him for an unforgettable performance in the 3-3 draw at home to Man City.

He matched the £50million-rated Raheem Sterling stride-for-stride, each of them also snatching a goal. It was a Tierney cross that set up Celtic's third goal, despatched by Dembélé. Europe was now aware of the star in our midst. KT himself was even moved to swap shirts for the first time (with John Stone).

The new manager had seen enough to offer improved contract terms – less than a year after KT had signed a new four year deal. The Irishman was in no doubt that KT was fundamental to his plan to deliver 10-in-a-row to Celtic. The unassuming Bhoy confirmed that he wasn't the only one to benefit from his new deal in the Tierney household: *"To be fair, my digs money has gone up slightly – but I don't mind that."*

He had time to reflect on his new status as an established first-teamer during an enforced three-month lay-off, which started in October 2016 when he underwent operations on an ankle and a shoulder.

This meant he missed the League Cup Final win over Aberdeen – but only in the sense he wasn't on the pitch.

He attended all the games he couldn't play in and sat among the Celtic support in the away fixtures. It was remarkable to hear his name getting chanted at the end of the momentous 4-3 win at Fir Park in December and to turn around and see him up in the top tier shaking hands and having his photo taken with fans.

Three weeks later and there were similar scenes outside New Douglas Park before the game as fans crowded round for the chance of a photo and a word. There are some who say that modern footballers are entirely divorced from those who pay into the games. Kieran Tierney is not the typical modern footballer.

When the season re-started after the winter break with a game against Albion Rovers in the Scottish Cup, KT again replaced Izaguirre in the first team. There was no doubt in the manager's mind as to who the preferred left-back was. This meant he was renewing the excellent partnership he'd developed with Scott Sinclair down the left side.

It also meant the rekindling of his 'bromance' with Patrick Roberts, the two having developed a friendship since the Man City player arrived on loan in January 2016.

It didn't take KT long to remind us of what we had been missing. He was Man of the Match in the 4-0 victory over Hearts on 29th January where he put in some great crosses and set up goals for both Sinclair and Roberts. Yet again he seemed to have benefitted from what would have ordinarily been a set-back through sheer willpower.

When the league title was clinched at Tynecastle on 2nd April it was KT who was to the fore of the player celebrations in front of a rapturous Celtic support. When the trophy was handed over on 21st May in another Hearts game, the North Curve were treated to the Muirhouse Bhoy, megaphone in hand, leading the singing and dancing to herald the arrival of 6-in-a-row.

This is someone who, in the space of just two years, has become a folk hero to Celtic fans. The incredible consistency of his performances in the Hoops had continued through to the Champions League and he was now also a fixture in Gordon Strachan's Scotland team also.

He has remained unassuming and down-to-earth while making this ascent into football stardom.

The title party continued into the night for the fans but for KT it was a Chinese take-away and soft drinks to celebrate: *"I knew at thirteen I couldn't do some things because it would affect Celtic and that's the club I always wanted to play with, I have always been cautious. My friends realise that and that it's in my best interests. I do probably have to do different things to my friends at times, but that's been the same all my life. I don't drink so when I'm out, we play pool, listen to music and just do normal stuff. I don't get any hassle. I have just never fancied alcohol. I don't know what will happen down the line, but I probably won't drink."*

There remained the unfinished business of a potential Treble. The Scottish Cup Final was a tough encounter, with Aberdeen determined not to be steam-rollered by Celtic the way they had been in the League Cup Final earlier in the season. The teams were all square midway through the first half when Aberdeen striker Jayden Stockley smashed an elbow into the side of KT's face. The young Celt stood in shock holding bloodied teeth and nursing a broken jaw.

It was a straight red card all day long (which would have been Stockley's fourth of the season). Incredibly he wasn't even booked. Kieran's final was over as he was rushed away for hospital treatment and replaced by Callum McGregor.

In his absence, the Scottish Cup was eventually won and a glorious Treble clinched, Celtic having gone the entire season unbeaten by any Scottish club. As the players went up the Hampden stairs to be awarded their medals, Patrick Roberts made sure that KT's contribution was not forgotten as he donned his pal's Celtic jersey with 'Tierney 63' at the front. It was a fine gesture of support for his missing pal.

For some people, there really is something inside so strong. KT was not to be denied his moment of glory. After the emergency treatment, he insisted on returning to Hampden. He then got caught up in traffic around the National Stadium as Aberdeen fans left in their droves following the final whistle. Jumping from his transport, he took to his heels (still wearing his full Celtic kit and boots!) and ran through the crowd and up the stairs at Hampden's main entrance. He made it – just – as the last of his Celtic team-mates were being given their medals in the presentation area. Looking shell-shocked while exchanging words with Lisbon Lions Willie Wallace and John Clark, he turned with the cup and his medal and his roar joined with the roar from the Celtic End as the support realised he'd made it back for the party after all. Back where he deserved to be. It was a defining image in a season like no other.

CHAPTER 8 — FEBRUARY
We didn't sign Denayer

WE DIDN'T SIGN DENAYER

BUT IT DOESN'T MATTER

COS WE SIGNED BOYATA!

1 FEBRUARY: CELTIC 1 ABERDEEN 0 ♇

The Dons arrived in Glasgow for this Wednesday night fixture with confidence high after a run which had brought them five wins in succession. Derek McInnes' team were sitting in third spot, two points behind Rangers although with a game in hand. They were encouraged by the fact that Celtic were still without a recognised striker with Dembélé and Griffiths still injured. Playing with a high line, they tried to turn Celtic's pressing game against them.

This approach met with some success as they prevented Celtic from scoring in the first half although we still had most of the scoring opportunities. Kieran Tierney almost got on the score-sheet when he spotted Joe Lewis off his goal-line but his attempt just cleared the crossbar. A Ryan Jack tackle was needed to prevent Scott Sinclair from opening the scoring.

As it had proved so often this season, it was just a matter of time for Celtic. And so it came to pass in the 57th minute that Dedryck Boyata outjumped the Aberdeen defence to head home a Sinclair free kick. The rejuvenated Belgian internationalist had won a second game for Celtic in the space a week and the fans were delighted for him. He was ultimately to be rewarded with his very own song from the support – which Kieran Tierney regularly sang in the dressing room!

In this most momentous of seasons, Celtic had again beaten our main rivals to reach the 67-point mark – and February had only just begun. Even when not playing as well as they could and not at full-strength, Brendan Rodgers' team could still get results. That was the mark of true champions.

5 FEBRUARY: ST JOHNSTONE 2 CELTIC 5 ♇

All roads lead to Perth this Sunday as Celtic, with a 25 point lead in the League, sought to make the gap unbridgeable. Saints were the last Scottish team to beat Celtic and clearly fancied their chances of derailing the Rodgers' bandwagon.

Liam Henderson's first Celtic goal in two years gave Celtic an early lead but a deflected header from Watson was followed by a Wotherspoon header which glanced off Boyata and past Gordon, meaning that Celtic went in at the break trailing 2-1. This was a proper battle we were in.

With the momentum in their favour, it looked as though St Johnstone might create an upset and grab all three points. Moussa Dembélé re-appeared in the Hoops in the 59th minute following his recent injury worries and, two minutes later, Tierney turned Foster inside-out then delivered a cross which hit off Watson's body. Referee Craig Thomson blew for a penalty, thinking it hit a hand. The anger of St Johnstone manager Tommy Wright post-match was sufficient to fuel Torness power station for a week.

Dembélé duly despatched the penalty and, with the equaliser in the bag, Celtic went in for the kill. Roberts set up the French striker for an easy shot from the edge of the box to give Celtic the lead on the 75th minute. Five minutes later, a Scott Brown clearance was seized on by Paddy Roberts who set up Sinclair to drive home a right foot shot past goalkeeper Clark. 4-2! What a comeback it was – but the Bhoys were not finished there.

Five minutes from the end, with the chant of "Here we go – 10 in a row!" reverberating all around McDiarmid Park, Celtic created a goal of bewildering beauty. Twenty-four passes involving every single Celtic player – and without an opponent touching the ball – led to Moussa Dembélé securing a second-half hat-trick in less than half-an-hour! Yet there was so much more to this goal. It was the essence of Brendan Rodgers' philosophy of football.

A move that started in midfield was foiled down the right wing yet Celtic held on to the ball, playing it all the way over to the left side and then, when that channel was blocked, playing it back through the defence to Craig Gordon. Patience was the key.

The game was won, no point in risking anything. The keeper's simple touch kept the move alive by bringing in Scott Brown who in turn introduced the unlikely lynchpin of this piece of perfect controlled football, Mikael Lustig.

The Swede played a 1-2 with Roberts, then did the same with McGregor before passing on to Dembélé then continuing his run to the left side of the St Johnstone box. Dembélé's pass to Lustig was then met with a Rabona (or as the guy next to me exclaimed *"A f**king Rabona for f**k sake!"*) from the Swede which took out one defender. The ball landed at the feet of McGregor who back-passed into the path of Dembélé who smacked it into the bottom left-hand corner of Clark's net.

This was football at its most glorious. I received a text on the way home saying Celtic's fifth goal had more passes than Kirk Broadfoot on Mastermind.

Celtic had yet again overcome adversity to claw back a deficit and emerge victorious by 5 goals to 2. This was the mark of true champions. The graffiti on the wall was absolutely bang on: *We're magic! We're magic!*

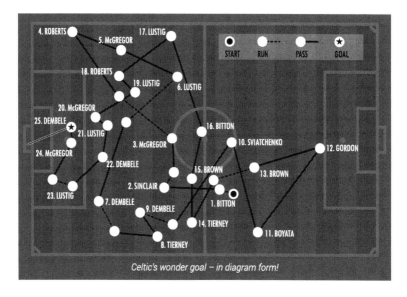

Celtic's wonder goal – in diagram form!

On the bus, it sounded as though Radio Scotland's commentary team were on suicide watch, so devastated were they by the penalty decision for Celtic's second goal. In a 5-2 defeat, it was strange that the loss of a single goal could be described as "the game-changer."

What is most bizarre is that, while on odd occasions referees deny our opponents a goal or award a penalty, we get denied actual trophies by refereeing decisions - and Scotland's broadcasters are rarely moved to comment.

It was soothing to hear the pain of mega-chinned clogger Paul Paton after the game. He bleated online: *"Could have been so much different today but bad decisions changed the game."* One Celtic fan responded: *"You're right about bad decisions – you should have been sent off."* He really should adopt Tony Mowbray's mantra and take it on the chin. It's clearly big enough.

There was some distressing news for Celtic fans a few days later when the reign of Warbiola ended with a whimper. Things had gone awfully mouldy for the man whom fans of The Rangers had greeted as the best thing since sliced bread. His leaving of Ibrox was a comedy of errors. The club put out a press release saying he had resigned. He then put out a press release denying this, maintaining he'd been sacked. It appeared as though The Deadies were attempting to avoid having to pay him any compensation by insisting that he'd walked away. It was pantomime season all over again at the Debtdome.

Even more amusing were the media's attempts to try and re-write history by painting Warbiola as a busted flush from the start, when they'd spent most of the season talking up his chances of taking the title off Celtic – and as a future England manager! The laughter continued when it turned out the interim manager, Graeme Murty, was rumoured to have been a Celtic fan in his younger days and had requested Celtic play in his testimonial game.

If the media quickly turned on Warbiola, it was nothing compared to the speed with which those who had previously worn 'magic hats' in his honour and had taken Warburton's bread-wrappers to their games turned on the man. He went from Messiah to Money-grabber quicker than you can say "liquidation deniers." Yet again the Gullibillies were dancing to the Level 5 tune.

Once bitten, twice ... bitten for ra Bares.

It was back to Scottish Cup duty and a home tie against ICT. There was now increasing talk of a potential Treble with the League Cup already won and an apparently unassailable lead in the League. The support's desire for a Treble was very strong, with Ronny Deila's recent attempt at winning this honour having been thwarted by honest refereeing mistakes. It had been fifteen years since the last time a Celtic manager had won all 3 Scottish competitions – and he happened to be an Irishman in his first season in charge at the club. The omens were good.

The omens were much less favourable for another Irishman, the ICT manager Richie Foran. It was a surprise that he was still in the job given that the Inversneckians had been rooted to the foot of the table for most of the season. Foran was also prone to heaping praise on his players one week, then slating them derisively the next. He displayed the kind of passive aggression normally associated with Mrs Doyle from Father Ted – and much of her tactical acumen.

Celtic had received bad news before this game when Tom Rogic, missing since late December due to an ankle injury, broke down in training. The popular Socceroo would likely be out now for a further 8 weeks while the ankle recovered.

This game quickly descended into a turkey shoot and it was no surprise that Mad Mental Mickey Lustig got the party started in the 20th minute when he ran onto a lob, controlled the ball in front of the ICT keeper – then nutmegged him with a side-foot pass into the net! On the stroke of half-time Forrest fed Dembélé and Fon Williams contrived to let his shot cross the goal-line.

Much more impressive was the Frenchman's finish for Celtic's third goal five minutes into the second half but that was surpassed when, ten minutes later, Dembélé won the ball in the centre circle, passed it out to Forrest (who put in an impressive shift overall), matched the winger's run through the centre and finished off a superb move with a delightful header from Forrest's cross.

It was his second hat-trick in successive games, third of the season, and he was finding his form at a great time for the team. He was also the first Celtic striker to score back-to-back hat-tricks since Henrik Larsson in 1999. And still only 20 years old.

There was a roar of celebration when Kieran Tierney netted his first goal of the season and Celtic's 5th with a bullet header into the roof of the net five minutes before the end of the match. The celebrations didn't end there though as Paradise was treated to its first 'Broony' in a while when the captain hammered home a loose ball beyond Fon Williams to make it 6-0 in injury time. James Forrest had 3 assists in this game making it 11 assists for the season, more than any other player. Brendan Rodgers knew there was a player in there and his decision to keep faith with Forrest was well rewarded – he was having a superb season.

This was a devastating, ruthless performance from Celtic – and the Treble dream was alive and well. It was difficult to believe that this Inverness team were the only Scottish outfit so far this season to stop Celtic taking full points from them.

18 FEBRUARY: CELTIC 2 MOTHERWELL 0   ♛

It was a familiar story at Celtic Park as Mark McGhee's Motherwell parked the bus in front of their goal - and invited Celtic to put their windaes in. The Fir Park team had shipped seven goals to Aberdeen in their previous game and were intent on avoiding another mauling.

Patience was once again the key for Celtic. A clumsy challenge in the box on Dembélé just after the half hour mark led to the Frenchman converting another penalty with ease. James Forrest was rampant once again and he assured a Celtic victory before the first half ended when he picked up a ball out on the wing, sent defender (and former Celtic team-mate) Joe Chalmers the wrong way, then drove the ball past Samson into the net.

Celtic confidently saw out the second half and preserved another clean sheet, the team's 12th in 14 games. Aberdeen were now a distant 27 points behind in second place.

The safe standing area in Paradise was now evolving into a safe dancing area. Each time the Scott Sinclair Song was sung, the fans in the North Curve crouched down for the first part of the song – and then went crazy, jumping up and down all over the shop, as it reached its crescendo. The effect this was having on the rest of the stadium was infectious. The marked improvement in the atmosphere this season owed much to this area of the ground as well as the team's performances.

There was jumping up and down of a different kind a few days later when the club revealed plans for a new hotel and museum to be built at Celtic Park. The Gullibillies were up in arms and foaming at the mouths when the story broke. One even referred to it as *"a council-funded museum for the Liams"* provoking much online mirth for Tims. Some claimed that the land had originally been worth £11 million (remember this is the East End of Glasgow, not the Hollywood Hills!) but Celtic had bought it for little more than half a million. It was sad to see paranoia reach such levels amongst a support who were swapping their Warbiola 'magic hats' for tinfoil headgear instead.

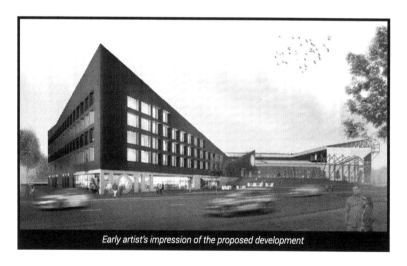

Early artist's impression of the proposed development

It was the turn of Hamilton Awfycomicals (as my wife insists on calling them) to revisit Celtic Park for this Saturday fixture and they proved to be as awkward opponents as their Lanarkshire derby rivals had the previous weekend. Although still mired in the relegation battle with Inverness, Hamilton appeared better organised and more tenacious than the Highlanders.

It took a moment of sublime skill from Moussa Dembélé to separate the teams on the verge of half-time. With his back to Donati, the striker turned him comfortably with a draw-back before flicking the ball – without even looking to see where the goal was – over the despairing keeper from all of 25 yards out. Celtic Park rose in acclaim of an outstanding demonstration of the striker's craft.

Kieran Tierney's drive into the heart of the Hamilton defence an hour into the game resulted in a penalty – and up again stepped that man Dembélé for his 29th goal of the season, the 8th he'd hit from the penalty spot. What a signing he had been.

This was Celtic's 21st successive victory in the league. The consummate professionalism with which each game was being approached was testament to Brendan Rodgers' emphasis on preparation as well as his man-management skills. We were reaping the rewards as it looked as though no team in Scotland could lay a glove on us.

CHAPTER 9 – MARCH
He scores belters all the time

BRENDAN SAID

I'M GONNA PLAY HIM IN CENTRE-MID

WORDS CAN'T DESCRIBE

WHEN I SEE HIM IN THE GREEN & WHITE

HIS HAIR IS FINE

HE SCORES BELTERS ALL THE TIME

THAT'S WHY WE SING THIS SONG

FOR STUART ARMSTRONG

It was another midweek trip up to the Highlands for Celtic's away support at the beginning of March. The Caledonian Stadium has been a difficult place to visit since ICT joined the top flight back in 2004 and this season was the only away ground that Celtic had not returned from with full points.

ICT's lowly league standing and the recent 6-0 thrashing in Glasgow suggested that history would not repeat itself tonight. As had been the case recently, it took until the stroke of half-time before a Celtic breakthrough was made. This time it was a bursting run and sumptuous finish from outside the box by Scott Sinclair that gave Celtic the lead. The song crafted in his honour was sung with gusto throughout the rest of the game. As was the legendary chant of *'The Huns are going bust – again!'* at half-time, back in the place where it was first aired five years earlier.

The second half had only got underway when an absolute clanger from Fon Williams led to Dembélé lobbing him and then tapping the ball into an empty net in front of the happy, well-wrapped up Celtic support in the South Stand. It was his 30th goal of the season and none had come easier for the French Under 21 Internationalist.

Stuart Armstrong was next to have the Celtic fans up in the air in celebration when he rattled in a direct free kick into the top left corner of Fon Williams' net. It was his 10th goal of the season and he was the 5th Celt to reach double figures as the goals kept racking up.

The last word went to Dembélé after a pinpoint pass from Tierney breaking from defence sent him scampering through on to Fon Williams whom he chipped with characteristic aplomb as the space was narrowing. The travelling Celtic support had been served up a veritable feast which went a long way to make up for the late equaliser conceded on the previous visit. Only 7 points were now needed to clinch 6-in-a-row.

There was widespread sadness the day after the Inverness win when it was announced that one of our greatest heroes, the club legend Tommy Gemmell, had passed away after a lengthy illness at his home in Dunblane. He was aged 73. It was especially poignant that Tommy had died so close to the 50th anniversary of the day when his goal against Inter Milan earned him fame throughout the world of football.

5 MARCH: CELTIC 4 ST MIRREN 1

Before the game there was a minute's silence in honour of Tommy Gemmell.

The Lisbon Lion with the big shot was also remembered through some excellent banners on display.

The visit of First Division St. Mirren for this Scottish Cup quarter final proved more hazardous than many of us had thought. After going ahead in the 13th minute and retaining the lead until half-time, the Paisley side – attempting to survive relegation after a disastrous start to the season - were certainly making things uncomfortable for us with a well-drilled 3-5-2 formation. Celtic had fielded the same eleven who had battered Inverness during the week but they were failing to make an impact. Gary Mackay-Steven did not make it out for the second half, replaced by Paddy Roberts, and he was one of the few players in the squad that Brendan Rodgers seemed unable to draw consistent performances from.

Seven minutes into the second half came what could have proved a remarkable turning point in Celtic's season. A St Mirren free kick into the box was swiped at by Dembélé, causing the ball to spin up and over Craig Gordon's head and on to the cross bar. Davis, the goalscorer, beat Boyata in the air to the rebounding ball but he couldn't divert it into the net. There was much exhaling of breath and swearing all around. If St Mirren had gone two up then maybe, just maybe, even this Celtic team might have struggled to recover three goals. Mikael Lustig equalised with a header in 58 minutes and a minute later it was time for yet another Scott Sinclair Special when he bent the ball around the keeper and into the net from just inside the Saints' penalty box.

The dam was burst: a brilliantly worked goal between Roberts, Sinclair and Dembélé made it 3. Ten minutes later, substitute Leigh Griffiths struck from 25 yards out for a convincing 4-1 victory.

Scotland's tabloid reporters worked themselves into a lather at Brendan Rodgers' post-match comment that St Mirren had proved the best Scottish team that Celtic had faced so far this season. This was taken as a slap in the face to Aberdeen and, particularly, to their darling Rangers. Yet the truth of the matter was that Jack Ross's side had come closest so far to de-railing Celtic's unbeaten run. They subsequently survived relegation too.

It had been 298 days since Celtic had lost a game to another Scottish team. The unbeaten sequence now read as follows: WWWWWDWWWWWWWWWWWWWWWWWWWWWWWWWW. There had been much wailing and gnashing of teeth in the mainstream media about Celtic's dominance which many considered 'unhealthy' for Scottish football. Many in the Celtic community reflected on how, when Oldco Rangers were this dominant during the 1990s, the papers were notably silent about the 'unfairness' of the situation – and none were calling for a strong Celtic to re-emerge to challenge them. Funny that.

One wag pointed out online, maintaining the domination theme, that *'Celtic like to dominate, whereas the club on the southside much prefer role play, pretending to be Rangers'*.

At a bookshop near you: 'Fifty Shades Of Complete Dominance' by Brendan Rodgers

33 points was the difference between the teams at the start of the day and it was largely due to Rangers' key danger man, referee Bobby Madden, that the gap hadn't widened. In the last minute of the game, Leigh Griffiths was chasing a long ball and was fouled by Clint Hill as they ran into the Rangers box. Griffiths remained upright and was about to unleash a left foot drive when Hill launched a waist-high challenge from behind which brought the striker crashing to the ground.

On any planet it was a penalty but not, apparently, on Planet Freemasonry. It should never have been left for yet another honest mistake to decide the outcome of this game though. While Celtic started off inhibited by Rangers' 4-4-1-1 formation which denied space, this had been the standard approach of small clubs coming to Celtic Park looking to steal a point this season. Celtic created opportunities as they always did yet the team appeared weary at times.

On two occasions Moussa Dembélé got in behind the Rangers' defence but he couldn't make it count. Gordon made a good stop from The Blue Lagoon-sponsored Waghorn before Stuart Armstrong almost put Celtic in the lead on the half-hour mark with a free-kick which came cannoning off Foderingham's left-hand post. Just a few minutes later though, Forrest worked the ball to Armstrong on the right. Taking a single touch, Armstrong drilled a stunning left-foot shot past three defenders and into the corner of the net, taking everyone by surprise. It was beautifully struck. Yet another great moment in an unforgettable season for the Aberdonian who had made himself an integral part of this Celtic team.

Early in the second half, further chances for Armstrong and Dembélé should have seen Celtic home and dry. In the 51st minute Kieran Tierney raised huge cheers with a brilliant nutmeg of Tavernier. Rangers were tiring, as so many other teams had, as Celtic's passing game wore them down. Armstrong again came close when he almost beat Foderingham from distance but the keeper managed to claw it away.

'The One True Faith' – North Curve pre-match display

Five minutes from time Dembélé had a golden chance to seal victory when Griffiths set him up. Despite turning Wilson, his shot flashed wide of the post.

The Rangers had their chances too and the Celtic defence, especially Sviatchenko, had looked uneasy at times. Three minutes from time, Gordon stopped a shot from Hyndman only for Clint Hill to squeeze the ball over the line. Their fans celebrated like they'd won the World Cup, the Ryder Cup and the Ashes (how appropriate!) all at the same time. Celtic could have – and should have – won it at the death but for the referee's wilful blindness of Hill's foul on Griffiths.

The plucky newcomers had stolen a point, only the second team so far to do so against Rodgers' team. It was reported that Club 1872 rushed out commemorative t-shirts to mark their special occasion.

19 MARCH: DUNDEE 1 CELTIC 2 ♟

A sunny Sunday afternoon at Dens Park saw Celtic on the cusp of claiming the League title. Dundee had improved their position since the teams last met, moving up to eighth in the league, but had had a miserable month. They were demoralised to see Celtic snatch the lead in the last minute of the first half, thanks to a deflected effort from Simunovic which he managed to get on target after great trickery on the wing from James Forrest.

Soon after the break Forrest was again involved when he skipped past a Dundee defender and floated the ball across perfectly for Stuart Armstrong to head home with ease. That should have been that but an unnecessary challenge from Boyata let in substitute El Bakhtaoui who unleashed an unstoppable shot over the head of Gordon. Marcus Haber then almost snatched a late equaliser but Celtic managed to see the game out. Dundee had again came close to stealing a late point.

Post-match, Brendan Rodgers talked of the pressure the team had brought on itself: *"There is a different competition in itself, to see who can maybe be the first team to beat Celtic. But we can only apply ourselves as well as we possibly can. I've told the players not to worry about headlines in terms of 'invincibles' or 'trebles'. My worry is just to play the best football we can, and if we do that, we will win games."*

It was an underwhelming performance but yet again, even when not performing at their peak, Rodgers' team had taken all three points. The unbeaten run now stretched to 36 games and only one more win was required for us to be declared Champions. It was time for another international break, meaning it would be April before the title could be won.

The gap in Celtic's schedule afforded one group of supporters the opportunity to pay homage to a famous Celt who is buried in Prague in the Czech Republic. Johnny Madden, originally from Dumbarton, played in the first ever Celtic team which beat Rangers in May 1888 and went on to lead the line for the club throughout its first decade. When his playing career was over Johnny took up an offer of a coaching position in 1905 with Slavia Prague. Over 3 decades as manager, Johnny turned Slavia into one of Central Europe's leading clubs and earned the moniker 'The Father of Czech Football.' He had married a Czech woman with whom he had a son and he remained in Prague through to his death in 1948.

The Celtic Graves Society organised a trip to Prague where, in association with Slavia fans group Odbor Pratel (Friends of Slavia), a memorial was held at Johnny's graveside in the Olšanské cemetery.

A large crowd of fans were in attendance to hear speeches about Johnny's life and career from Slavia and Celtic fans as well as members of Johnny's family.

At Johnny Madden's graveside

Later in the year, Slavia fans persuaded their club to name one of the stands at the Eden Arena after Johnny, a fitting and lasting tribute to a Celt who became such an important sporting figure in a country many, many miles from Dumbarton.

CHAPTER 10 — APRIL

Glasgow's Green & White

CELTIC [CELTIC]
CELTIC [CELTIC]

COME ON YOU BHOYS IN GREEN
[COME ON YOU BHOYS IN GREEN]

COME ON YOU BHOYS IN GREEN
[COME ON YOU BHOYS IN GREEN]

GLASGOW'S GREEN & WHITE
[GLASGOW'S GREEN & WHITE]

GLASGOW'S GREEN & WHITE
[GLASGOW'S GREEN & WHITE]

When Hearts finally get around to opening their new Main Stand at Tynecastle they should consider naming it after Scott Sinclair as the Celt has enjoyed more highlights on that ground that anyone wearing maroon in recent years. It was no real surprise then to find Sinclair again to the fore when the chance arose to clinch the League title on Hearts' turf – they might even have considered marking him a bit more closely.

The downside to potentially winning the League at this ground was that the away support allocation in the Roseburn Stand has been restricted to 1400 in recent years (not including the forgeries of course!). Tickets for this game were more scarce than a Rangers fan on University Challenge.

Brendan Rodgers' stated aim in taking the Celtic job was *"to win in the best way we possibly could."* On this day, when Celtic were forced through injury to play without a recognised striker, his Celtic team turned that mantra into football gold in the Gorgie sunshine:

24: Scott Sinclair plays a one-two with Roberts on the edge of the box then smashes the return pass into the roof of the net.

27: A Lustig pass is dummied by McGregor to run free to Roberts who brilliantly evades a tackle and splits the defence with a pass that Sinclair runs on to and right-foots with ease past Hamilton.

55: Tierney passes inside to Roberts whose dummy allows the ball to run through to Armstrong who glides into the 'D' and hammers the ball home.

61: McGregor presses on Nowak and wins possession before his left-foot slides the ball beyond the defender into the on-rushing Roberts who collects, dribbles then clips the ball past two defenders and Hamilton into the far side of the goal.

84: Sinclair takes a pass from Tierney, slips between two defenders to race into the box where he is brought crashing down by Nowak – then hits the resultant penalty high into the net to claim hat-trick.

Five goals. A clean sheet. Champions of Scotland.

My heart was pounding with pride at a Celtic team clinching a sixth league title in succession with such brilliant, positive free-flowing football. It was the style of play our club has historically been associated with. In a pleasant historical footnote, Scott Sinclair's third was Celtic's 9000th League goal.

Brendan Rodgers and his players were creating new Celtic history with a style reminiscent of the past but thoroughly modern in its execution. And it was magic!

The Joy of Six in Paradise

After the title was won, there was some hilarity from a familiar corner albeit with a new face. The new manager of The Rangers, Pedro Caixinha, decided he'd announce at a press conference what his team would be before their next game – and managed to leave out a goalkeeper! A day later he made the statement (clearly spoon-fed to him by an overweight PR guru) that: *"We have a culture of winning and getting the three points all the time."*

This was brave talk from a team who were trailing Aberdeen in third place in the league. The Gullibillies had a new leader – and he was already proving to as much of a figure of fun as Warbiola had been.

The Champions were warmly welcomed back to Paradise the following Wednesday and the Partick Thistle's players formed a guard of honour as Mikael Lustig led the Celtic team out. Scott Brown was given the night off and in his place the £3 million Kouassi started for the first time.

The only difficulty with winning the Title as early as Celtic had just done meant the team were left with eight games spare which could prove meaningless. Yet there was still the challenge to keep the unbeaten run going until the season's end and fight for places in the Scottish Cup semi-final against Rangers towards the month's end. Would that be enough to keep defeat at bay?

Thistle certainly had plenty to play for. This was proving to be their best season in years and they were looking to claim a spot in the post-split Top 6 for the first time. Having only lost two league games since the turn of the year, they came to Celtic Park with plenty of optimism. They again proved a difficult team to beat. It was only on the 50th minute when their defence was breached. Roberts and Sinclair combined superbly, the Man City loanee threading a pass through the defence which Sinclair slid past the oncoming Cerny to give Celtic the lead.

The Celtic support was delighted to see Tom Rogic return from injury after a four-month absence, replacing Kouassi midway through the second half. Thistle were undaunted by Celtic's lead and equalised on the 64th minute after Azeez breezed a shot past a snoozing Celtic defence at Gordon's front post. A foul on Gamboa in the box gave Scotty Sinclair the chance to win the game from the penalty spot late on but Cerny saved his low strike. Thistle could have grabbed a shock win after Erskine sent Azeez through but Celtic's defence finally managed to clear the danger.

The unbeaten run was intact and Thistle were only the third team this season to take any points off the Champions. Would anyone else emerge to spoil the record-breaking sequence?

The day before this Kilmarnock game, Celtic fans received unexpectedly good news. After winning the league in his first season and with the Treble a distinct possibility, Brendan Rodgers signed a new contract which committed him to the club for four years (rather than the one year rolling contract agreed the previous summer). It didn't take a Rachel Riley to work out that this meant he could be here to guide Celtic to the much-coveted record of 10 league titles in a row. Just when you thought things couldn't get any better...

The Scottish media greeted the news as warmly as a jobby in their lunch box. One reporter even despairingly asked the Celtic manager at the press conference: *"Do your friends in England ever ask why you're here?"*

Although there was little at stake in this game for Celtic, it was another strong team that Brendan fielded. Dembélé, Rogic and Kouassi all made late appearances as the manager worked through his options for the Scottish Cup semi-final which was now two weeks away.

The SPFL's Player of the Month, Stuart Armstrong, gave Celtic the lead 22 minutes in with a raking drive from distance which went through a ruck of players to beat Killie keeper Woodman. Celtic were comfortable throughout even after a deflected shot squared the game on 65 minutes. A tap-in for Scott Sinclair and a rare header from James Forrest secured a further three points for the Celts.

The best moment of the day came when Brendan, as he always does, took to the field to congratulate and speak to the players, and applaud the fans for their support. The Green Brigade had trialled a new tune in the North Curve that day that would quickly become a Celtic anthem: *This is how it feels to be Celtic...* As the manager applauded the fans in that ground, and as the line *Brendan Rodgers – here for 10 in a row* was sung to the rafters, he put his ten fingers up in the air in celebration just as the fans were doing.

Later, when pressed on it at the media conference, Brendan joked he was merely stretching his fingers. He gets it. He's here for The Ten. He knows it. We know it. They know it.

Before the Killie game, the Celtic FC Foundation and the Glasgow North-East Foodbank had appealed for fans to bring donations of food with them to be dropped off at various points outside Celtic Park. The idea was, after previous recent foodbank collections at the ground, for a range of different foodbanks throughout Glasgow, Lanarkshire, Ayrshire and Renfrewhire to benefit from the generosity of supporters. The appeal took place close to the anniversary of Brother Walfrid and his charitable spirit, at the heart of the club's identity, was evoked to encourage more donations.

The response was impressive. Over eight tonnes of food and dry goods were donated which filled 17 vans to benefit 17 foodbanks. In addition, over £3,000 was received in cash donations which the Foundation used to provide 400 lunches for homeless people at Celtic Park on Walfrid's anniversary on April 18th. For many, the idea of people having to use foodbanks in the 21st century is a national scandal.

While the need exists, it is good to see that football fans – often derided in many quarters – are consistently among the first to help out others. Celtic fans especially.

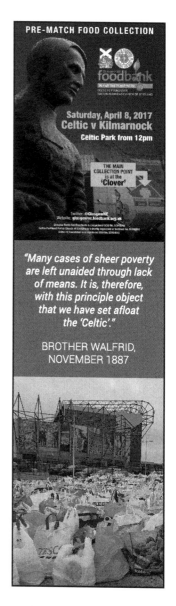

PRE-MATCH FOOD COLLECTION

foodbank

Saturday, April 8, 2017
Celtic v Kilmarnock
Celtic Park from 12pm

THE MAIN COLLECTION POINT is at the 'Clover'

Twitter: @GlasgowNE
Website: glasgowne.foodbank.org.uk

"Many cases of sheer poverty are left unaided through lack of means. It is, therefore, with this principle object that we have set afloat the 'Celtic'."

BROTHER WALFRID,
NOVEMBER 1887

The final trip to the Highlands this season proved to be a controversial affair. This Sunday fixture got off to a great start with a magnificent strike from Kieran Tierney from all of 30 yards. County equalised in the second half from an excellent header from former Celt Michael Gardyne before Paddy Roberts once again showed his class, nut-megging his marker and another defender before beating keeper Fox. There was little over ten minutes left but this game was only coming to life.

There seemed no danger at all as Erik Sviatchenko pulled out of a tackle on Alex Schalk in the Celtic box in the 90th minute. You could see all the way back in Glasgow that there had been no contact at all and the Dutchman wasn't going to hoodwink anyone with such a feeble attempt at cheating. Step forward Don Robertson.

The irony of Scottish referees being sponsored by Specsavers has never appeared in such sharp focus. He didn't bother to take the opinion of his assistant, who had a much better view of the incident than him, and awarded a penalty that Liam Boyce stuck away to tie the game at 2-2.

It matters little that Schalk subsequently accepted a two-match ban for his act of cheating or that our esteemed referee subsequently phoned Brendan Rodgers to apologise. It rankled badly at that time and especially with Scott Brown. The first opportunity to get a tackle in on Boyce and Brown cleaned him out. It was silly and unnecessary - but beautiful all the same!

Don Robertson didn't hesitate in getting his red card out or even consider whether a caution might have sufficed – well, there was a semi-final against Rangers coming up, wasn't there?

The red card was subsequently reduced to yellow on appeal and the appeal itself meant that the Celtic captain would feature at Hampden the following Sunday. There was a kind of justice in there, somewhere.

It was back to Hampden to decide who would face Aberdeen in the final but for Celtic it meant much, much more. The Treble was now within virtual touching distance.

Callum McGregor knows all about the significance of these games. As an Easterhouse boy who's been associated with Celtic since the age of 9 it couldn't be any different. The spur in his development under the new manager has been a joy to watch. While he still lags behind Armstrong and Rogic in midfield selection, his contribution to the Celtic cause has been considerable. None more so than when, eleven minutes in, Dembélé teed up the ball for him and he passed it around both Wilson and Foderingham into the net from 20 yards. The skill – and the temperament – deserved to be marvelled at.

Rangers fans had an early chance to cheer when Dembélé pulled up with a hamstring injury in the first half. His enforced absence meant that Leigh Griffiths came on to spearhead the Celtic attack. They weren't laughing for long. It was a bursting run from Griffiths that drew Tavernier into making a crazy lunge just inside the box to stop him. Even Willie Collum had to give a penalty for that (although no red card, despite the fact Griffiths had been denied the clearest of goal-scoring opportunities). Up stepped Scott Sinclair and he hit it with just enough power to get past Foderingham, who got a hand to it. Early in the second half and the tie was over bar the shouting.

Martyn Waghorn passed up a decent late chance for a goal. But no-one, genuinely, expected anything less from the tubby Englishman. In one magnificent comedy cameo he had chased after a pass all the way down the left wing and beyond the bye line, without even coming close to catching it. It was like watching Dumbo On Ice.

Tom Rogic almost provided the icing on the cake in the dying seconds with another exquisite shot from distance which beat the keeper but not the post. All in, this proved another blissful Hampden in the Sun experience for the Celtic faithful.

Go Home ya Huns! rang around Hampden and the great unwashed duly obliged: having lost four games out of five to Glasgow's big team this season, they proved yet again that they were world champions at walking away.

One of the best and briefest match reviews ever came from an online Sevco fan following this semi-final. Horrified at the suggestion his team might provide a guard of honour to the new Champions when they stepped out at Ibrokes the following weekend, the angry Bear vowed: *"I'm handing my Rangers scarf in if we give them a guard of honour. It was bad enough we let them pish in our mooths at Hampden for 90 minutes."*

29 APRIL: RANGERS 1 CELTIC 5 ♆

This was the kind of day that would inspire Lou Reed to write a song about it. It was perfect in every sense.

It had Scott Brown, which was one of the many things about this day that drove the Bares to despair. His Ross County red card rescinded, the Fifer helped direct one of the most memorable Rangers humiliations that either of their clubs have experienced. It was a pass from the captain that set Patrick Roberts haring into the Rangers box only for Myles Beerman to bring him down needlessly.

It had Scott Sinclair. Who else would you rely on to step up and wrongfoot Foderingham with the penalty to get the party started just 7 minutes in?

It had Leigh Griffiths. Some within the support had under-estimated for a while just how high quality a marksman he is. Increasingly this season, when given the chance, he demonstrated his uncanny eye for goal and the spectacular. Being preferred for the younger Dembélé must have caused him concern but he buckled down. Today was one of the days he got his reward. When Armstrong sent him through down their right side in the 18th minute there was no obvious danger. Or so they thought. But Celtic's No. 9 is a natural born driller. He took one look up and hit the ball with such ferocity that Foderingham's two hands couldn't stop it powering past him into the netting. He then took a wander over to the corner flag for a rest. As you do. No Dembélé? No problem!

It had Jozo Simunovic. Putting Kenny Miller in the air. With a tackle that became iconic.

It had Callum McGregor. Who else would you want to nutmeg Tavernier on his way to scoring Celtic's third goal then jumping up and down in front of the Broomloan mirroring the mass hysteria on show in the stand?

It had Joey Garner. When he came on as a sub in the 57th minute the Celtic support mocked him by chanting *"You've got (clap clap) Joey Garner"* at the few remaining Sevconians who hadn't left the ground. Yet.

It had Kieran Tierney. Because while we used to dream about this kind of regular mauling in the Glasgow Derby, for KT our dreams are his reality. And he will have many more days like this to come against them. The bhoy is blessed!

It had Dedryck Boyata. It had to. While resurrecting his career after grafting into the early hours in the gym to get back in the first team, he was scoring headed goals for fun and winning Celtic games on this glorious, undefeated run.

There was no-one better to get on the end of a Griffiths free-kick in the 66th minute and head it through the legs of the sprawling Foderingham. Mind the Gap indeed.

It had Kenny Miller. Well, every good live show has a cameo from a clown at some point.

And it had Mikael Lustig. A Mental Mickey Lustig cameo to beat all cameos. There he goes, winning the ball in the centre circle. Taking it for dander, right through the heart of the Rangers midfield and defence. Riding challenges, swivelling those hips. And when he was finished, switching feet and bending the ball around Foderingham's desperate, grasping right hand. To make it five. FIVE!!! And off he goes again, Hoops over his head, sliding along the front of the Broomloan and taking a remarkable bow from his adoring public. What a man!

The pre-match controversy over a guard of honour was forgotten as Ibrox stewards ended up guarding their goalposts from another scarf being placed there by Leigh Griffiths. As the Celtic players partied in the goalmouth in front of a disbelieving support, the rest of Ibrox emptied faster than Neil McCann's bowels after receiving a payment notice from HMRC.

It was a game that had everything. Rangers 1, Celtic 5. Our biggest away win at Ibrox since 1897. The first time a Celtic team had scored 5 goals there since our first-ever visit on 27th October 1888 when Celtic ran out 6-1 winners in a Glasgow Cup tie.

This season proved without a doubt, whether it was the East End, Hampden or the Crumbledome itself, Glasgow was Green & White. That chant, uproariously sang between the bottom and top tiers of the Broomloan, summed it up wonderfully. It echoed around the three silent stands of Ibrox packed full of fuming, impotent liquidation-deniers. It was yet another reminder that they were not Rangers anymore.

They don't do walking away, they claim. On Saturday 29th April 2017 they ran away.

THE GOLDEN BHOYS

50th Anniversary of the Lisbon Lions

It began with a few blinks of light. Then a chant started in the junction of the North Stand and the Lisbon Lions Stand and grew stronger and louder throughout the stadium:

IN THE HEAT OF LISBON
THE FANS CAME IN THEIR THOUSANDS
TO SEE THE BHOYS BECOME
CHAMPIONS
SIXTY ♥ SEVEN

It was a scene replicated in the 67th minute of every Celtic home game in season 2016-17 and more than a few away games too. It was at its most spectacular in evening matches at Celtic Park when the whole stadium was glistening in light thanks to thousands upon thousands of camera phones, held up in tribute. It was a carnival of light and sound celebrating the greatest team in both the history of Celtic and of Scottish football.

Fifty years on, the achievement of Jock Stein's Lisbon Lions remains undimmed. The first non-Latin team to be declared Champions of Europe who won the Big Cup in a style that has rarely been repeated in the intervening five decades. It was that style, that emphasis on attacking flair as opposed to dreary defence as perfected by Inter through their notorious catenaccio (bolt) system that made the greatest Celtic manager ever so proud of what happened on the 25th May 1967: *'We did it by playing football. Pure, beautiful, inventive football.'*

A new Celtic Supporters Club in Bray, Co. Wicklow, Ireland – named after the greatest of them all

Many of the supporter stories that abound about that trip to Lisbon have themselves gained legendary status. One of those concerned a 'motorcade' of cars travelling in convoy from Celtic Park all the way to the Estadio Nacional. Celtic fans Martin Coyle and Barry Sweeney decided to recreate the journey and, to make it a truly authentic experience, they re-built a Hillman Imp (built in 1967 in Linwood – and incredibly re-discovered in Portugal of all places), painted Hoops on it and christened it Jinky!

Jinky heads to Lisbon yet again

A film crew joined them for the trip and, despite a few scares along the way (the car caught fire before leaving Glasgow) wee Jinky made it to Lisbon in time for the big day.

Another group of Celtic fans took the same road as Jinky but theirs was a more arduous endeavour all round. A team of 28 cyclists set off from Celtic Park on 11th May 2017 and travelled through four countries for over 1,300 miles (including up and over the Pyrenees!) and arrived at the Estadio Nacional on the 25th May.

They raised the magnificent sum of £73,616 for three charities in the process.

The Road to Lisbon – complete!

Numerous Celtic fans made the pilgrimage to Lisbon during the course of the anniversary season. Thanks to the efforts of supporter David Mitchell, there is now a permanent reminder of Celtic's glorious day at Estadio Nacional itself. David liaised with the stadium authorities in Lisbon as well as Celtic to persuade them to have a plaque installed on the stadium wall to remember the events of 25th May 1967 and the victory over catenaccio.

John Clark unveiled the plaque on Thursday 27th April 2017 and said:

"We have visited the stadium many times and now when we, or our supporters, return again it will be fantastic to see the plaque in place as a record of that wonderful day.

Like myself, I know all my other team-mates will be delighted and humbled by this gesture."

It was estimated that over a thousand Celtic fans journeyed to Lisbon to be there on the anniversary day itself. Many partied long into the night at Rua Nova do Carvalho (the famed 'Pink Street) the night before where, bizarrely, a policewoman on duty there turned out be the sister of '90s Celtic striker Jorge Cadete.

A few made it to Mass the following morning at the Basilica of Our Lady of the Martyrs where Glasgow priest Fr. Charlie Cavanagh was the celebrant-in-chief. The focus of the celebrations was the old stadium itself, largely unchanged after all these years. The Portuguese FA allowed Celtic fans to visit the stadium for two hours even though it was being prepared for the Portuguese Cup Final just two days later.

Throughout the array of events organised by the club and supporters to celebrate this golden anniversary, the Lions themselves were well represented. The evergreen and unique Bertie Auld was more often than not centre-stage, often with Jim Craig, John Clark and Bobby Lennox alongside him.

Celtic fans in Bobby's hometown of Saltcoats used the anniversary as the springboard for a fundraising campaign to build a statue of Buzzbomb in the seaside town which met with a great response from the wider support. Willie Wallace made the journey back from Australia in May for the main events. Unfortunately Stevie Chalmers, the man whose golden touch sealed the win in Lisbon, was unable to attend any events due to ongoing ill-health. Given that this group of heroes are in their late 60s and 70s they are of course susceptible to all that old age entails. It was with great sadness yet courage that Billy McNeill's family made the announcement in February that the mighty Cesar had been diagnosed with dementia.

Tragically a bigger blow was to come.

On Thursday 2nd February 2017, Tommy Gemmell passed away. The much-loved Celt, renowned for his great character as well as the rare feat of scoring in two European Cup finals, had been unwell for a long time. Yet the news still came as a shock to the support and, of course, his great friends among the surviving Lions.

Tommy follows Bobby Murdoch, Ronnie Simpson, Jimmy Johnstone, Joe McBride, Willie O'Neill – and, of course, Jock Stein, Sean Fallon and Neilly Mochan – from the ranks of Celtic's greatest team whom we have now lost.

The CSC from the town of Dunblane, where Tommy spent the latter part of his life, unveiled a unique memorial banner of Tommy at Celtic Park the following Saturday. His is a light that will never go out.

There was truly only one show in town in Glasgow on 25th May 2017. A sell-out 13,000 crowd at the Hydro on the Clydeside witnessed a superb night of entertainment led by Rod Stewart and great Celtic figures from the past including Martin O'Neill, Kenny Dalglish, Gordon Strachan and Neil Lennon who all came to pay homage to the Lions as did their old foe, Alex Ferguson. Glasgow truly was green and white on the 50th anniversary of Celtic's glorious triumph.

To make sure there was no doubt that Glasgow belonged to the Lions on this golden anniversary, various sites throughout the city had been emblazoned with life-size copies of the classic image of Cesar lifting the Big Cup. It was a lovely reminder of Scottish football's greatest achievement for everyone in the city to enjoy.

The club got in on the act as well. On the night of 24th May a number of prominent advertising sites throughout Glasgow were taken over with official Lisbon celebration billboard posters proclaiming '50 years ago, eleven local Bhoys became LEGENDS.' It was a touch of class.

By far the most spectacular celebration of the Lisbon Lions during this golden anniversary year came in the last home game of the season, the week-end before the anniversary itself.

Before the Hearts game, the Green Brigade organised a display funded by the wider support and which was brought to life by a capacity Celtic Park crowd. Arguably the best ever choreographed display in a football ground on these shores. The effect was mesmerising.

The quality and impact of this Lions display – and the work that went into it – were acknowledged later in the year when Celtic supporters were awarded the Fifa Fan Award 2017 for the *"stunning 360-degree card display around Celtic Park to honour the Lisbon Lions"*.

The season-long celebrations were a tremendous gesture of support and gratitude for the men who brought undreamt-of glory to our club.

One scene brought home for me the fact that the achievements of the Lisbon Lions will always be recognised. Before the last home game of the season against Hearts, I was standing with my son at the top of The Celtic Way a good thirty minutes before kick-off. We were surprised when spontaneous applause broke out in the crowd around the main entrance. Brendan and the players had already arrived some time before.

The mystery was revealed through brief glimpses of a white-haired man, assisted by his wife Liz, making his way to the front door of the stadium. It was Cesar. The initially respectful applause (there were no shouts) was thunderous by the time he made his way up the steps into Celtic Park itself. The response from the supporters to the great man was truly heart-warming.

The Lions themselves still marvel at the adulation that keeps coming their way. On the anniversary day itself Jim Craig said: *"It's just amazing to get the reception that you get from people who've never met me before and they've always got a story to tell. It's been a real privilege to go through your life as a Lisbon Lion because you meet people from all walks of life and they just want to meet someone who played in that game. It's been absolutely fantastic. The Celtic fans are a special bunch, and we count ourselves very lucky that they've kept us so close to their hearts."*

The golden star that sits atop the Celtic crest and the Main Stand at Celtic Park will forever be testament to that wondrous, shimmering afternoon under the Lisbon sun – and to the men whose ground-breaking achievement lit up our lives.

CHAPTER 11 — MAY
This is how it feels

THIS IS HOW IT FEELS
TO BE CELTIC
CHAMPIONS AGAIN
AS YOU KNOW
BRENDAN RODGERS
HERE FOR 10 IN A ROW!
[10 IN A ROW]

The season had come down to this: five games in May that would decide whether this Celtic team would earn the title of 'Invincibles' for a campaign without a single defeat in domestic competition and also win an historic fourth Treble.

The first obstacle was St Johnstone at home. Tommy Wright's team were looking to claim fourth spot in the league for the third season in succession, an impressive achievement. They were doughty opponents again. When Paddy Roberts put Celtic in front with a 25-yard drive early in the second half, they responded immediately with an equaliser (Steven MacLean again celebrating a goal against Celtic as if his season ticket renewal at Ibrox depended on it).

Once again it was the redoubtable Boyata forehead that restored Celtic's lead from another Griffiths corner. Patrick Roberts soon snatched a third before Callum McGregor, just on in place of Rogic, tackled, twisted and turned past four opponents in an incredible run over 40 yards before stroking the ball home sweetly from just beyond the penalty spot.

This game saw a debut for Mikey Johnston on the left flank and the return of another 18-year-old, Anthony Ralston, who'd made his debut the previous season. Both acquitted themselves well and it was great to see more Celtic youths stepping up into the first team. Brendan Rodgers took them both to the North Curve at the game's end to earn the deserved acclaim of the standing section and the wider support.

Scott Sinclair, who had been the victim of foul racist abuse in the 5-1 molligation at Ibrox, was shown solidarity with the display of a banner that proclaimed *'Anti-Racism is Beautiful, Magical'*. At the game's end he accepted a t-shirt from the Green Brigade emblazoned with the slogan *Love Celtic – Hate Racism*.

Three more points, four more goals. Still undefeated.

And so to Pittodrie, home of our closest challengers in the League (now 9 points clear of Rangers in second place) and the team who were waiting for us in the Scottish Cup Final in a fortnight. The cynics among us felt that if the unbeaten run was going to come to an end, it would likely be here, on a foggy Friday night, by the North Sea.

Thankfully, cynicism was one of the earliest casualties of the new Brendan Rodgers' era. It was more a case of 'Wherever we go we fear no foe' and Aberdeen away held no fears for this team. The game was over in 11 minutes. That was all the time it took for Celtic to put three goals past a shell-shocked defence.

Dedryck Boyata kept up his incredible run of headed goals with a cracker just 3 mins in. Ash Taylor was cast aside with ease as the big Belgian rose brilliantly to head home yet another Griffiths corner.

The Celtic support in the South Stand then had a wonderful view of a Griffiths' nutmeg on Reynolds which was the prelude to Stuart Armstrong firing home from close range. On his way to taking the plaudits from the jubilant Jungle Jims, the big Aberdonian found time to blow a kiss to some old friends in the Dick Donald Stand.

Two goals up with only 11 minutes on the clock it was time for Celtic's striker to get in on the act also. Despite the attentions of both Taylor and Reynolds, Griffiths found the space to turn, look up and – from fully 25 yards out – smash the ball into the net. Devastating. The Celtic fans were on their feet again celebrating a third goal after only 660 seconds of play. They'd had more exercise than the Aberdeen forwards by this stage.

Even though Johnny Hayes pulled one back a minute later and Aberdeen missed a bundle of chances (and Steven McLean, remarkably, passed up a chance to send off Craig Gordon) Celtic went on to record their best result at Pittodrie in six years.

Even better, the team had had now reached the 100 points mark. The Scottish record of 103 points, set by Martin O'Neill's Celtic in 2001-2, was now in this team's sights. Could there be more history in the making?

100 points up at Pittodrie and the joy is unconfined

The Dandy Dons weren't too downtrodden though. The following Wednesday they travelled to Ibrokes Park and recorded a victory there for the first time in 26 years. It was a good thing that Rangers weren't alive to witness it.

The last away game of the season saw Celtic travel across the city to Firhill. It was a sun-kissed Glasgow evening which only enhanced the fantastic display of Lisbon-era fan banners which the BHOYS/ SMV group had organised in the Jackie Husband Stand – a week before the 50th anniversary of the great day itself. Some of the banners even went on to make a cup final appearance at Hampden.

Patrick Roberts used the occasion to showcase his talents. He was brought down in the box by Booth early in the game and Griffiths converted the penalty – Celtic's 100th goal of the season. Griffiths then turned provider for Rogic to score a second 26 minutes in. Cerny was beaten by an exceptional Roberts drive from outside the box just before half-time – and didn't reappear for the second half. Thistle's hopes of a first win over Celtic in 23 years disappeared also.

The party was in full swing in the away end in the second half. In fact, it was 10 minutes from the end and the support were singing *"Come on over to my place"* when an excellent run from McGregor finished with a dipping shot with hit the underside of the bar and crossed the line before ending up in substitute keeper Ridgers' hands. The linesman confirmed it was a goal and McGregor himself seemed surprised. TV footage established it had definitely crossed the line.

There was no doubt about Celtic's fifth though. The Huddle was going on in the Husband Stand when Roberts intercepted a pass outside the Thistle box, dragged the ball back and away from his marker before bending it majestically up and around the out-stretched hand of Ridgers. It was another bit of magic from a player who had gilded Celtic's season with his skill.

The only bum note on a memorable Maryhill night was Leigh Griffiths mouthing off at the manager when he was subbed in the second half.

Brendan Rodgers, while at pains to play down talk of a rift, made it clear who was at fault: *"For a minute he forgot himself. For a minute he thought about himself instead of the team. This is a team that is selfless."*

As the match was closing some Celtic fans were chanting We're going on the pitch! We're going on the pitch! but Thistle's elderly stewards put up a show of strength that their defence could only dream of.

In the Heat of Firhill – a superb old school banner display at the Partick game

After Celtic clinched 6-in-a-row for the third time in the club's history, the Celtic Graves Society held an event at St Conval's Cemetery in Barrhead to remember one of the lynchpins of the first 6-in-a-row side – that of 1905-1910, managed by Willie Maley. Joe Dodds formed part of the famed Celtic back-line of Shaw, McNair and Dodds and was a member of the 4 in a row team of 1914-1917.

A Celtic captain and formidable defender, Joe won an incredible eight league winner medals in 351 league appearances for the club.

A large crowd turned out to listen to Celtic historians and family members recall Joe and his wonderful career. The family produced a Scotland cap which they still retain which Joe received in 1914. The event was an excellent reminder of the richness of Celtic history and the many great characters who made the club a success from its earliest days.

The 38th and final game League of the season. Our sixth annual trophy presentation as Scottish Champions in succession. Back in the mid-1990s this level of success for our club was impossible to imagine. Then we went six years without winning a single trophy and nine years without winning the league. Here we were, older and wiser, and on the cusp of a magnificent achievement: to go the whole season within a single defeat in the league. Arsenal had done it in 2004; Juventus in 2012. In Scotland it hadn't been done since 1899 – but the competition lasted only 18 games then. A win or a draw would mean this had been a unique, invincible season.

First things first though. This week was the golden anniversary of the club's greatest achievement. In honour of the Lisbon Lions, the Green Brigade had organised a whole stadium card and flag display – and it was spectacular. Each of the four stands at Celtic Park had a different design and, with the participation of the entire support, it came to life brilliantly: the image of the big cup in the Jock Stein Stand; a golden star emblazoned with '50' in the Lisbon Lions Stand; '1967' all across the Main Stand; and a flowing script with the legend 'Lisbon Lions' from one end of the massive North Stand to the other.

The amount of work that goes into the preparation of a display of that size is something else and the Green Brigade's members and helpers – as well as the crowd at Celtic Park who made it work – ensured that the 50th anniversary was celebrated in Paradise in magnificent style.

There was then the small matter of a football match. Since taking over as Hearts manager Ian Cathro had watched his team fail to find consistency and drop down into fifth place in the league table, not far above Partick Thistle. Given that this Celtic team had put five past them without reply at Tynecastle just a few weeks earlier, their chances of spoiling the party seemed low.

Hearts proved sturdier opponents this time round with Celtic generally restricted in the first half to shooting from distance. The visitors almost took the lead when a strike from Tziolis just flew over Craig Gordon's crossbar. At half-time it was 0-0 and Celtic needed to move up a gear to ensure the unbeaten record lasted until the League's end.

Five minutes after the restart, that man Roberts went flying down the right wing, gave Smith the soft shoe shuffle to get past him, and floated across a beautiful ball between the two central defenders that Griffiths headed home with ease. On the 76th minute, it was an excellent burst down the right from Griffiths that set up a chance for Sinclair which was blocked before Armstrong hooked the loose ball into the roof of the net. 2-0 for the Hoops.

It was party time in Paradise as the League trophy was handed over to Scott Brown for the sixth successive year.

With this sixth league title came the honour of the 'Invincibles' label. One man with an air on invincibility about him is Kolo Toure who had proven a popular – and, at times, key – figure over the course of the season. He had now earned the unique distinction of having gone a whole league season unbeaten twice – the first time with Arsenal's famed team of 2003-4.

It was the end of an era for Kris Commons, who took his place among his team-mates for the trophy presentation for the last time. Brendan Rodgers had some kind words to say to the popular Celt when addressing the stadium post-match before he expressed thanks to the people who matter most: *"Celtic is nothing without the support. We, as players, managers and coaches are on the field here, but what makes Celtic iconic is the people in the stands and the people all over the world."*

His Celtic team had just established a remarkable series of records which included:

TITLE WON WITH MOST GAMES TO SPARE (8)

BIGGEST TITLE WINNING MARGIN (30)

HIGHEST NUMBER OF GOALS (106)

HIGHEST NUMBER OF WINS (34)

BIGGEST POINTS TALLY (106)

FEWEST DEFEATS (0)

A season like no other — and it wasn't finished yet.

Cup Final morning - there are few better feelings. I get as excited about Celtic appearing in the end-of-season showpiece at Hampden in my 40s as I did when attending my first Cup Final aged 14. And today was to prove to be among the most memorable Hampden experiences of all.

I've made my way to Hampden through various routes down the years but this was the first time I'd done it as part of a corteo of a few thousand Celtic supporters winding its way from Glasgow Green across the Clyde and through the Southside to the National  Stadium. Despite the over-zealous policing which appears the norm at Celtic and other matches these days, the fans enjoyed a noisy sing-song and the odd flare moving along Aitkenhead Road. It certainly added to the sense of occasion.

After having beating Aberdeen five times already this season, including a straightforward 3-0 win in the League Cup Final, there was a lot of confidence about this game. Every Celt in the stadium and watching it on TV or online knew the importance of the game and that we were on the brink of history. Few expected Derek McInnes' side to perform as well as they did.

From the go, it was clear this was a different Aberdeen team and they were up for it. They pressed Celtic hard, got stuck into our midfielders and made a nuisance of themselves. They were clearly mindful of the recent Pittodrie match where an early Celtic barrage effectively won the game in the opening eleven minutes. They had also learned from their timid performance at Hampden exactly 6 months earlier. It was they who made the breakthrough in the 9th minute, with future Celt Johnny Hayes hammering home first time from a corner by ex-Celt Niall McGinn after it cleared everyone else in the penalty box. This wasn't in the script.

It had been 27 years since Aberdeen last won the cup. Bad thoughts were beginning to gather. The red half of Hampden was bouncing. Celtic needed an immediate response.

Step forward Stuart Armstrong. Straight from kick off, Celtic moved the ball forward. Callum McGregor tried to escape the attentions of two opponents but was fouled. Referee Madden played the advantage and the ball was knocked along to Armstrong, in front of the Aberdeen box. He gathered the ball with his right, surged forward and – just before Logan arrived to block – belted the ball clean into the far corner of the net with his left peg. An immediate equalizer!

This was a brilliant response as Aberdeen had built up a head of steam. Yet we were still only at the start of an enthralling encounter. Despite the set-back, Aberdeen kept coming. Hayes was threatening again on the wing. Shinnie, bursting through, almost beating Gordon but hit the side netting. And then Kieran Tierney was down on the ground, the side of his face having been smashed by Stockley's elbow. It looked bad all the way from the Celtic End. Aberdeen had certainly been mixing it yet, incredibly, referee Madden took no action at all regarding the blatant elbow which had broken the young Celt's jaw. The worst was confirmed when the substitute sign went up and KT got helped off the pitch. He'd missed the last Cup Final and only lasted for 25 minutes in this one.

Rogic came on and McGregor moved to the left-back spot. This was not what Celtic had wanted. Aberdeen continued to press hard. Gordon had to make a block save from McGinn and then he got down superbly to stop a long-range shot on the turn from Jack. A header from Stockley brought out another great stop from the Celtic keeper. Aberdeen seemed to be creating all the chances. We just needed to keep them out for now, then rally.

It was only in the last few minutes of the match that Celtic seemed to get a hold of the ball and create a chance. The Dons fans were whistling like mad to encourage the referee to blow for half-time. The ball fell to Griffiths who whipped in a deadly cross into the goalmouth and there was Sinclair, flying in to meet it, but the connection wasn't right and it went over the bar. At last, this was more like it.

A bleak outlook at Hampden

Aberdeen started the second half strongly. Griffiths managed to get close with a deflected shot and then Jack came close at the other end. Shooting towards the Celtic End, a brilliant chipped pass into the six-yard box from Rogic was met by Sinclair who tried to squeeze the shot under Lewis, but the keeper was able to get down and block. That was a real chance.

Things were more even now, with Celtic showing a greater presence. Yet, just after the Sinclair chance, McGregor got caught in possession by Hayes who sprinted away down the wing. With McGregor on his trail there were only two players in the middle: Brown and McLean. Brown had to move towards Hayes and, just then, the Irishman passed it square towards McLean who was one-on-one with Gordon. Our hearts were in our mouths as it looked more or less an open goal – but the Hayes' pass was too strong and it passed McLean as he tried to steer it into the net. What a let-off!

Now, Celtic were finally able to get decent possession – and Roberts on the ball. He teased Reynolds before stepping to his left and hitting a beautiful left-foot strike which came crashing off the post. At last, we had something to cheer. And then our momentum started to build - a foothold in the game, finally.

Lustig almost struck lucky when the ball fell to him from a corner. A Rogic run led to Roberts darting through the right side of the Aberdeen defence and his inviting cross was cleared over the bar by Taylor. THIS was what was needed. The noise from the Celtic End resounded around the stadium.

A Griffiths corner kick was centred superbly and Boyata escaped his marker to meet it flush with the head – but it flashed over. Still we came at them. Into the last 15 minutes and a beautifully-floated ball from Griffiths, after he snatched back possession, found Sinclair alone near the back post with just Lewis to beat – but he failed to meet it properly, the ball catching under his foot, and Aberdeen survived again.

Ten minutes left and Celtic were attacking as relentlessly as the heavy rain falling on the Hampden pitch. Chances came the way of Rogic, Roberts, Griffiths and even Lustig but all failed to either find the target or beat Lewis. The effort from the Celts was exceptional and Aberdeen were hanging on by their fingertips. In the 89th minute Rogic and Roberts combined to set up Sinclair but his shot on the turn was skied as he started to fall. All around there were hands on heads as it looked as though the final chance to win it in regulation time had slipped away.

Three minutes of injury time were announced. Great endeavour by Griffiths a minute in resulted in Celtic being awarded a corner. Everyone was on the tips of their toes in anticipation but Lewis managed to punch it away. That's it. Extra time was imminent. The Treble was truly on the line after a dogged Aberdeen performance. We were bossing the game now but they only needed a single goal to smash our dream into pieces. Players on both sides looked exhausted.

A Craig Gordon clearance was won by Armstrong who passed it out right to Rogic. In front of him were Roberts, Griffiths and Sinclair – all marked. O'Connor went to meet him – Rogic jinked then beat him for pace and drove into the box. Considine stood in his way but the Australian – juggling the ball between his feet – glided past him. He'd ran almost 40 yards and now only goalkeeper Lewis was between him and the goal.

It looked like he'd slightly over-ran it, the angle didn't favour him. His right foot stretched to connect with the ball as Lewis started to dive. From Row N in Area G1 of the Celtic End it looked too tight an angle. The ball went past Lewis but was it going inside the post?

The net shook, the ball nestled in the corner – and Rogic headed off towards the fans in the Main Stand clutching at the Celtic badge on his shirt. The outpouring of noise was astonishing.

It was a moment that will always live with me. All around, fans are jumping and hugging and screaming and falling. Arms and even some legs are flailing. I get caught up in the beautiful carnage, almost dragged back into the row behind as fans grab anyone and everyone to hug and embrace. Those who don't know football or Celtic can never understand that THIS is what is all about as a supporter. These moments are truly priceless. I notice a man in the row in front of me standing completely motionless – both arms aloft – struck still by the importance of what his eyes have just seen.

This is OUR moment in history. No Celtic fans who have come before us have witnessed a Treble being secured in such a dramatic fashion. We are the only people to see a Celtic team go undefeated in every domestic competition for the whole season. We'd seen it done with style, some truly glorious goals and a passion to match our own.

THIS is how it feels to be Celtic...

"The strength of Celtic,
and this is where we can be different,
is that real bond and connection
between that holy trinity of players,
the management and supporters.

When all three are together
you can really see the strength
you can gain from it.

And Celtic's a very, very powerful club.
That feeling, that connection that you have.
If we have that and we stay strong together
then we can go on and achieve
many more great memories."

Brendan Rodgers – July 2017

CELTIC FOOTBALL CLUB

AFTERMATH — 27th May 2017 — McChuill's Bar, High Street, Glasgow

Five hours on from Tom Rogic's Trebletastic goal and the party was showing no sign of easing up in one of the city's best known Celtic boozers. Auld Nick, mine host and DJ, was keeping the crowd entertained with his famed eclectic mix of tunes and the occasional Celtic anthem.

In among all the drinking and dancing and singing I got talking to a guy from the table next to ours who was out with his wife and her pal. He was telling me about the game. He couldn't get a ticket so watched it at home in Blantyre. *"Nervous as f*ck"* was how he described the experience. Celtic's failure to get the breakthrough second goal was driving him to drink but their dog — a tiny shih tzu — was driving him to distraction, barking and howling at him as he paced up and down the living room, letting out one agonising cry after another as Celtic were getting closer and closer but the winning goal still proved elusive.

To calm it down and enable him to watch the game without interference he had to sit down on the sofa and let the dog sit on his lap. He then had to keep stroking it to keep it subdued. This was working like a dream – the shih tzu was calm, he was controlling his emotions and his shouting, the second Celtic goal looked like it could happen at any moment.

The chances kept coming. He managed to stay seated and the dog remained passive with the incessant stroking and the occasional belly rub. He thought extra time was inevitable, the clock was running down. And then Rogic got the ball. As he moved closer to the Aberdeen goal everything seemed to stop. He was in on the keeper. And then, as the ball went under the keeper and into the net, he let out an almighty roar – and threw his arms into the air. Having forgotten that that he'd been holding the dog in his hands since the Rogic run had started.

In his own words, *"the dug got f*cked off the living room chandelier"*, his wife started screaming and the dog was making crazy noises of its own – but he only had eyes for Tom Rogic and their telly as he jumped up and down in front of it.

It wasn't as bad as it first sounded. The chandelier was plastic, not glass. The dog was shaken but not hurt. Dozens of shiny plastic shards now littered their living room floor. His wife was still going crazy. But Celtic had won the Treble and the dog hadn't died – what the hell did he care?

THIS is how it feels to be Celtic...

ACKNOWLEDGEMENTS

Ritchie for his inspirational design work and layout. Archie for his expert editing skills. Brendan for tremendous insights and advice. Jim, Fergus and the Oompah Kings. Super Ally fae the Glens. Leftybhoy. Frank. The CGS bhoys. Patrick & The Loveable Eejits, the Diaspora's most desperate and delightful sons. Dessie and those undimmed Andalucian dreams. Larry for the bible belt background. The mad couple in McChuill's.

Mya & Finn, the best sweetie-munchers and swearing monitors in all of Paradise.

Gill for everything – and more. You'll Never Walk Alone. ❤

Read more Celtic scribbles at **www.theshamrock.net**, home of the Celtic retro magazine.

You can find out more about some of the Celtic supporter initiatives and groups mentioned in the book here:

www.celticgraves.com

www.thekanofoundation.com

www.ultras-celtic.com

25334135R00103

Printed in Great Britain
by Amazon